The Anti-Entrepreneur

10 Strategies to Get Promoted and Retire Wealthy Without Starting Your Own Business

By

Staci McIntosh

This is a work of nonfiction. Nonetheless, some of the identifying characteristics of situations and persons involved have been changed. Any resulting resemblance to persons living or dead is entirely coincidental and unintentional.

The information and advice provided in this book in no way guarantee future employment or promotional opportunities. Similarly, financial, retirement, and savings information relies on hypothetical scenarios. You are never guaranteed the returns or results provided in such scenarios.

For professional advice regarding your specific financial situation, see a professional, certified financial planner.

Copyright © 2018 Staci McIntosh

All rights reserved. This book or any portion thereof may not be reproduced or used in any manner whatsoever without the express written permission of the publisher, except when appropriately cited and attributed to the author.

Published in the United States by Sensible Solutions
Henderson, Nevada

ISBN: 9781720013983

Table of Contents

About the Author	v
Introduction	1
Strategy #1: Work Harder Than Everyone Else	3
Stand Out Among Your Peers	4
Get A Degree, Or Two	8
Keep Learning	12
Strategy #2: Exude Executive Presence	18
Look Like a Professional	19
Mind Your Manners	23
Strategy #3: Be Trustworthy	27
10 Ways to Develop Trust	28
What Not to Share About Yourself	32
Listen More Than Talk	33
Strategy #4: Choose the Right Boss	38
10 Characteristics of the Right Boss	38
How to Handle a Difficult Boss	42
How to Leave a Bad Boss	47
Strategy #5: Think Like Your Boss	51
How Does Your Boss Think?	51
What Does Your Boss Worry About?	56

Strategy #6: Be Strategic About Mentoring — 62
- How to Ask for a Mentor — 63
- How to Be a Good Mentee — 65
- How to Have a Safe Mentoring Relationship — 69

Strategy #7: Connect Up, Across, and Down — 74
- The Networking Web — 74
- Connect with Influencers — 79

Strategy #8: Use Multiple Connection Strategies — 82
- Verbal Connection Strategies — 83
- Non-Verbal Connection Strategies — 85
- In the Moment Connection Strategies — 87

Strategy #9: Maintain Your Professional Relationships — 89
- Maintain Professional Friendships — 89
- Maintain An Active Online Presence — 92

Strategy #10: Be Your Own Retirement Planning Expert — 96
- Choose Your Preferred Retirement Lifestyle — 98
- Choose Your Retirement Option — 101
- Follow the Dos and Don'ts for a Wealthy Retirement — 112

Conclusion — 122

Want To Know More? — 123

About the Author

Staci McIntosh has nearly 20 years of experience as a Human Resources executive in both public and private sectors. She has worked for organizations ranging from 4,500 to 80,000 employees and has interviewed or coached over 1,000 individuals. Staci believes in helping people navigate the invisible rules and networks that make career navigation easy for some and difficult for others.

Staci writes her books with one goal: improving opportunities for all people to achieve their dreams. Through her brief, easy-to-read books, she provides ambitious, hard-working people with simple tools and straight-talking advice designed to expand and elevate their career opportunities. Staci sees the potential for each person to succeed, even if they don't yet see it in themselves.

Staci entered the workforce as a teacher and assistant principal. After discovering her love for Human Resources, Staci held roles as a Director, Executive Director, Assistant Superintendent, and Chief Human Resources Officer. She is currently the Vice President of Human Resources for a popular casino resort on the Las Vegas Strip. Staci holds a bachelor's degree from Eastern Washington University, a master's degree from Whitworth University, and a doctorate from Washington State University.

Staci's hometown is Spokane, Washington. She now lives with her husband Jim in Henderson, Nevada. Together they own Sensible Solutions, a consulting company devoted to providing practical resources for busy organizations and people. They enjoy eating great food on the Strip, binge-watching TV series, traveling to beach resorts, and spending time with Jim's teenage son Ben (an expert level Xbox One player) and Staci's daughter Kendall (a busy human resources professional).

Introduction

Being your own boss. Setting your own hours. Reinventing yourself. Escaping the shackles of 9 to 5. Living the startup dream. These phrases probably sound familiar to you. But they're not what this book is about. This book is the opposite.

This book is for the Anti-Entrepreneur. This book is for people who don't want to risk their life savings, their retirement plans, and their medical benefits to start their own business. This book is for people who realize that most businesses fail.

This book is for people who want to get promoted and make more money. It's for people who don't mind working for someone else. It's for people who want to retire earlier than their friends and colleagues.

But can you retire wealthy, even early, working for someone else? Are there career strategies to ensure it happens? The answer is yes! This book provides you the tools you need to do so. In it, you will learn ten very important habits to ensure career advancement and early retirement—without starting your own business.

Like a steady paycheck? Want a promotion? Want to retire earlier than your peers?

Read this book. In it, I give you practical career strategies that will greatly increase your promotion opportunities while decreasing your risk of being unemployed. Then, I explain how to leverage your promotion money into a wealthy retirement, however you define it.

Are you ready to take steps toward giving yourself the promotion you deserve and the retirement you want? Let's get started!

Strategy #1: Work Harder Than Everyone Else

Many people think that the only way to work harder is to stay late at the office. That's one way of course. However, working late at the office isn't do-able for everyone. And it can certainly be a problem for parents of young children who are in day care.

The concept of working harder than everyone else is as much about perception as it is about the work itself. You want to cultivate a hard-working persona to your boss. You want to cultivate that same persona to the gatekeepers in your organization. Gatekeepers are those with formal or informal power to help or hurt your promotion chances. You want your boss and the other gatekeepers to see you as reliable, dependable and motivated.

Being seen as the hardest worker has several advantages. The obvious advantage is that you will be more strongly considered for promotions. Another advantage is that you are likely to be favored for special assignments that will improve your career brand and hence your future opportunities.

Being the hardest worker also makes you more likely to be chosen to work on cross-functional projects. This will give you visibility to stakeholders in other departments, which will in turn open your career opportunities in other parts of the organization. An added benefit is that making connections with people outside your regular work group is a form of networking. Having positive relationships with diverse peer groups helps provide a pathway toward your upward mobility.

There is also one very practical reason to be the hardest worker. This is that you are less likely to be laid off. If your company experiences economic difficulties, they need to keep the employees who can take on the highest number of multiple assignments. If you're known as someone who can juggle a lot of assignments at once, you're more likely to be chosen to stay.

This chapter explains the variety of ways you can ensure your boss and other stakeholders see you as one of the hardest workers on your team. Do none of them, and you'll be seen as just another average worker. Do all of them, and your career brand will be greatly enhanced. The results of your efforts will bring you future job opportunities. Those will increase your salary. And when your salary increases, it will allow you to save more and retire wealthy.

Stand Out Among Your Peers

It's not enough to have a strong work ethic. In order to get promoted, your commitment must stand out among your peers. Achieving high sales volumes, leading a big project, and getting the best customer reviews will always get you noticed. But there are other, smaller, ways that will also help.

Below I've listed ten easy strategies to ensure your name will be mentioned the next time a promotional opportunity or high-profile project becomes available.

1. Respond quickly to requests. No matter who is doing the requesting, respond quickly. But you should also prioritize your time to ensure that those with the most power—formal or informal—get what they need from you right away. If the request will take you a few days to complete, tell the requestor when you expect it to be done. Explain why it will take a bit longer than anticipated. Then deliver it sooner.

2. Stay late with the boss. When you know the boss is staying late, make every attempt to do so yourself. The benefit of this strategy is twofold. First, your boss will notice your work ethic and commitment. Second, it's an opportunity to connect with your boss. Outside the busy workday, you'll get more one-on-one time. If your boss is a workaholic who puts in twelve-hour days, choose some of the days to stay late with him. For single parents dealing with daycare, this takes planning. You'll need to schedule the days you plan to stay late. And you'll need to rely on friends and family to occasionally pick up the kids.

3. Attend optional work functions. At any job, there will be optional work events. These include conferences, seminars, charity events, or award ceremonies. You should prioritize your attendance at these events. Yes, you'll probably be busy and yes, they typically aren't very interesting. However, if multiple colleagues and bosses will be there, you'll want to seize the opportunity to connect. After you attend several, people outside of your regular work group will get to know you. That will help your name stand out if an important work opportunity arises.

4. Attend work-related social events. You might think that attendance at social events wouldn't help you stand out among your peers. And yet it does. This is because chatting with work people in a less formal environment

helps you connect. And when you connect, you make a good impression. And then you stand out. Obviously, your attendance at social events won't make up for an otherwise lackadaisical work ethic. But when combined with the other strategies, it can be a powerful tool to get your name out there. Regardless of your interest level, force yourself to attend birthday parties, baby showers, weddings, and any informal occasions where multiple colleagues and bosses will be socializing.

5. Volunteer as an organizer or leader. Be the person who volunteers to take care of those little extra projects no one wants to do. When your leader asks, "Who will volunteer to take this on?" raise your hand, unless it's totally outside your area of expertise. In organizations, volunteers are usually needed to help with technology adoptions, communication cascades, training, and small event planning. Even if you hate doing whatever is being requested, try to contribute at least something. You can say, "This isn't really in my wheelhouse so I can't lead it, but I would be happy to help by…."

6. Share your expertise with others. This is one of the very best ways for you to develop name recognition in your company. Reflect on your strengths. Then look for opportunities to help others develop theirs. Be the person others go to for help or advice. Note that you cannot be seen as a know-it-all. And obviously, you cannot divulge sensitive information. What you want is to be the name mentioned when someone says, "Who could help me think through this?"

7. Never turn down an assignment. If you prove yourself by doing great in your regular role, you'll probably be asked to take on assignments outside your normal responsibilities. You should say yes unless doing so will

impact your ability to perform in your regular job. And, if the assignment will advance your name recognition with a new group of colleagues, you should do everything in your power to prioritize the offered assignment. Even if you have to work more from home or in the office, your commitment to helping out for the greater good will be commended.

8. Answer and initiate email on weekends or after hours. You don't need to totally ignore work-life balance in order to make this strategy work for you. But you do want others to recognize that you are willing to work outside regular hours. It helps you advance if people know they can rely on you to take care of required business regardless of the day or time. Make it a habit to check your email on the weekends. Also make it a habit to initiate email on the weekends. To limit the impact on your personal life, set a time limit. For example, spend 30 minutes (or only as needed) in the morning and 30 minutes in the afternoon either initiating email or responding to it. People will notice your time commitment and your attention to detail.

9. Stay late, or stay up late, to finish projects. There are going to be situations when a deadline looms and you don't have enough time in your day to get done what you need to. If you've committed to completing a task before a specific deadline, you must do whatever it takes to get it done. Most of the time, you won't need to physically be in the office to complete it, which is helpful if you need to get home to your kids. Under those circumstances, take the project home. It's worth it to lose a few hours' sleep to maintain your image as a person who manages deadlines well, even in the midst of a heavy workload.

10. Recognize special occasions. Some people never remember their colleagues' birthdays and anniversaries,

let alone set time aside to get a gift. If that is you, then develop a strategy to help. Even if you personally don't care if your boss recognizes special occasions, be aware that most people do. And when you take the time to recognize others, it helps your reputation. You will be seen as a hard worker who cares about others and who takes the time to make positive gestures on special occasions. One of my best friends buys greeting cards in bulk. She looks at whose birthdays are coming up, and she signs cards for each individual. Then she gives them to her secretary to manage the timing of when each card gets sent. It probably takes her less than an hour per month to write the cards, yet it results in an enormous amount of good will and respect for her professional brand.

Get A Degree, Or Two

Look at the high-level leaders who hold the jobs you aspire to in your organization. What degrees do they have? In most professions where you work for someone else, you'll need a college degree to advance more quickly. In addition, plenty of research will tell you that people with degrees, on average, earn more money over the course of their careers. In fact, if you grew up poor, getting a degree is the most impactful way to permanently get out of poverty.

But be warned. You won't use most of what you've learned from a higher education. Rather, having at least a bachelor's degree becomes more of a gatekeeper. Even if you don't need the knowledge you'll gain to advance, not having one will prevent you from advancing.

This will be even more true if there are many competitors for the position you want. The reason why is that when a company has 50 people apply for the job, they need to narrow it down somehow. If everyone has about the same level of experience, then the degree becomes the tie-breaker to determine who might get the job. The degree shows your employer that you have the perseverance, motivation, and grit to tackle a hard task and complete it.

You can certainly find experts who will say you don't need a degree to earn a lot of money. The problem with that advice is that it focuses on outliers, not the average. If you start your own business and are really successful, why go get a degree? I agree. But the odds are against you. Most new businesses fail.

In any organization, you'll find a few highly-compensated leaders without a college degree. But count how many. Probably not a lot. And they most likely began with the company when it was small. If you want to increase your chances of getting a job or a promotion throughout your entire career, get a bachelor's degree.

When we were in our twenties, my ex-husband Steve got a degree in teaching. He couldn't find a job right away, and we were poor. He needed to work. He ended up being hired by a company who told him that his bachelor's degree was what got him the job. What was the job? Inside sales for a roofing products supply company. Steve quickly started earning more than a teacher's salary. Then he leveraged that job into a better one at another roofing supply company, received stock, was bought out by a larger company, and ta-da! His retirement account was fully funded by the time he was 45. For sure, get a bachelor's degree if you haven't already.

But what about an advanced degree, like a master's degree? Unless your profession requires an advanced degree, as is the case for doctors and lawyers, that's a little more tricky. In deciding whether or not to get an advanced degree, it's helpful to understand the way the compensation system works in most large companies. Usually, there is a compensation department. In that department, people evaluate how much a job offer is going to be. An advanced degree isn't going to automatically catapult you into a higher job offer. But the degree will help boost the amount if you're switching companies. Your hiring boss might need to make an argument to the compensation department to get you more money than you made in your previous job.

In addition, having an advanced degree will make you more competitive if you need to switch companies and are looking for a new job. It's not going to take the place of work experience if a rival candidate has a lot more. But it could be the deciding factor regarding who will get the job and who will not.

Did I convince you to get a bachelor's or advanced degree? If so, use these parameters below to find a convenient program at the lowest cost possible.

1. Ask about tuition assistance at your company. If your company supplements or pays for certain degrees or degree programs at local universities, access one of those. If your company will pay for your degree, it's a no-brainer to get it, and to get it through their program. It would be a waste of money for you to pay a different university for a different program. Tuition money is money you could be using to fund your retirement. Avoid it if you can.

2. Avoid expensive universities with sexy names. Sure, it's great to say you went to Harvard or Yale. But if you're paying for it yourself, attending a famous university isn't necessary. Once you get outside the education sector, very few employers will care where you went to school, as long as it's been accredited by a respected accrediting agency. Find accrediting agencies on the United States Department

of Education website, www.ed.gov.

3. Avoid for-profit universities. These are businesses. They need to earn money, and thus their tuition costs tend to be quite high. They might be high-quality, but there are plenty of cheaper options. There are private and public schools that offer a great educational value for your tuition dollars. The bottom line is, shop around. Various publications rate universities on the value of their education relative to tuition costs. Just search for lists providing "best private university value" "best public university value" and "best value online degrees", or other criteria you are looking for.

4. Use on online option. These days online options have lost the stigma of being a much easier route to a degree. Those who are working while earning their credentials find online option extremely convenient. In the past, a single mother might have found it too difficult to get a degree because she couldn't leave her kids at home. Not any more. Conservatively, I recommend you pursue an online option with a university that also has an in-person component. The reason why is that more traditional hiring managers may still disregard a university that works primarily online, even if it's accredited. Almost all major public and private universities now offer several degrees through an online option. If convenience is important to you, and if you're a motivated person who works well independently, an online option is the best bet for you.

5. Save and pay cash as you go. Do not take out loans in order to get your degree, unless you absolutely have to. Instead, force yourself to go on a more limited budget during the time you're in school. Consider moving to a place with cheaper rent, or driving a less expensive car. And if funds are really short, find the cheapest accredited

university program you can. In most cases, getting your degree isn't going to provide instant return on investment. You'll still need to work hard to get that promotion. You'll need to wait until one becomes available. Don't sideline your money goals by getting a loan you'll have to pay back while making the same salary you do now.

6. Avoid diploma mills. A diploma mill is a business pretending to be a college. They lure you in with promises that you can complete a bachelor's or master's degree quickly, with very little effort. Make sure your college is accredited by one of the national, respected accrediting agencies listed on the United States Department of Education website, www.ed.gov.

7. Analyze the return on investment for getting your degree. Not having a degree can be an impediment to your career advancement. But what if you're in your forties or fifties and you're likely to end your career in the job you have? In that case, getting a degree may be a poor choice financially. Remember, you want to get your degree to help you access multiple career pathways. The younger you are, the more likely a degree will help your career advancement for multiple promotional opportunities. The older you are, the less likely this is to happen. Go ahead and get a degree in your fifties if it has been your dream to do so. Just don't think it's going to provide a huge return on investment at that point in your life. You must consider that you might be better off using tuition money to save for retirement.

Keep Learning

Be the person who stands out by mastering key concepts contained in the most popular leadership books. Whenever I mention this strategy in groups, I can see people thinking, "Books? I barely have time to do my work, let alone read books!"

If every time you read a leadership book, you fall asleep, I have a secret for you. I love reading, but I too had a hard time finishing leadership books. Then my husband introduced me to audiobooks. I began listening to business-related non-fiction in the car during my commute. I have a short drive to work, but it is amazing how many books I can complete in a month. I end up buying the hard copies of the ones I find particularly useful, so I can go back and reference them when I need to.

Audiobooks are more expensive than regular books, but don't worry. There are plenty of ways to reduce, or even eliminate, the price. You can reduce your costs by getting a subscription to a company like Audible. For about $15 per month, you get three audiobook credits each month. That usually gets you three books. If even that sounds too expensive, your local library has a large array of audiobooks as well. Just get yourself a library card and let them show you how to set up access.

The list below provides a baseline of fourteen leadership strategy books that have been read by thousands of leaders. Many books on the list are well over ten years old and have stood the test of time. To stay current, you'll want to read whatever is popular at the moment as well.

If you're not sure where to start, these will get you going. You can find them in short book summary versions as well. The books are listed in no particular order. Just start with the one that seems the most interesting to you and go from there.

The 21 Irrefutable Laws of Leadership by John Maxwell. Consider this a primer for basic leadership qualities. I read it again when I feel a bit stuck as a leader and need a refresher. John Maxwell is one of the most popular leadership authors, and you'll find something valuable in any of his books that you read.

Good to Great by Jim Collins. This book focuses on company characteristics but is applicable to individual leader skills as well. As the title suggests, the main point is that "good enough" is the enemy of great. If you apply that mindset to your own work habits, you'll find your career advancing at a quick pace.

Primal Leadership: Realizing the Power of Emotional Intelligence by Daniel Goleman, Richard Boyatsis, and Annie McKee. If you haven't heard of emotional intelligence, then you need to read this book. Daniel Goleman is the original researcher who began the emotional intelligence push. In this book, he explains why it's so important for leaders to exhibit empathy, self-awareness, collaboration and other "soft" skills in order to be effective.

The 7 Habits of Highly Effective People by Stephen Covey. I literally do not know any experienced leader who hasn't read this book at some time in their life. These simple habits are easy to understand and easy to implement if you are focused. They'll help you be an effective leader while managing your overall life and well-being.

The Five Dysfunctions of a Team by Patrick Lencioni. This is a short book told parable-style. Lencioni presents a fictional team of colleagues and uses their process to explain the behaviors and habits that derail group productivity. Unless your job is a completely solo effort, this book will help you lead teams and keep them on track.

The 48 Laws of Power by Robert Greene. This is the only book I strongly recommend only reading the summary version. It's long and tedious with plenty of references to Greek politicians and successful war leaders. The best parts are the laws themselves. They give you great tips for getting ahead without being seen as arrogant or threatening to others. Some of the advice is Machiavellian, explaining how to detail with your enemies. Some "laws" might be seen as unethical. Nevertheless, you'll learn a lot about managing and controlling office politics.

Crucial Conversations: Tools for Talking When the Stakes are High by Kerry Patterson and Joseph Grenny or *Difficult Conversations: How to Discuss What Matters Most* by Douglas Stone and Bruce Patton. I've included both titles because Crucial Conversations is considered to be the gold standard on this topic, but I actually found Difficult Conversations to be more practical. Either one will help you greatly. Even the most experienced leaders have difficulty giving bad news or making statements they know will generate anger or dissent. Both of these books provide strategies regarding how to structure the conversation. Use the tools to practice with your spouse or teenager, and you'll be a pro in no time.

Presence: Bringing Your Boldest Self to Your Biggest Challenges by Amy Cuddy. Of all the books I've listed, this one verges on the edge of self-improvement the most. But I felt it should be included because so many aspiring leaders fail to exude the confidence they need. The reason Cuddy's advice is so valuable is that it's easily achieved by any one. The strategies she gives to connect better and exhibit more confidence boil down to "power posing" which she explains in detail, along with the research behind it. After reading this book, you'll be telling yourself and your kids to "Starfish up!" before any high-stakes situation.

How to Win Friends and Influence People by Dale Carnegie. This is probably the most famous book regarding how to influence others. In it, Carnegie gives proven strategies that will help you lead others. You'll learn how to get people to do what you want without them feeling manipulated.

The New One-Minute Manager by Ken Blanchard and Spencer Johnson. An updated version of the hugely popular original, the book uses a parable to explain three of the most important leadership characteristics. It's a short, easy-to-understand book that has influenced thousands of business leaders.

When: The Scientific Secrets of Perfect Timing by Daniel Pink. I could actually recommend any book written by Daniel Pink, but I found this one particularly useful. It's the newest book on my recommendation list. Read it to gain practical strategies regarding the importance of paying attention to timing. When you start a project, when you interview, when you give bad news—science has all the answers regarding when you'll get the best outcome.

Smarter Faster Better: The Transformative Power of Real Productivity by Charles Duhigg. You'll feel more productive after learning the eight strategies in this book. It's incredibly well-researched and filled with scientific findings. Duhigg keeps it interesting by telling real-life stories of highly successful—and of course productive—individuals and groups.

Getting Things Done by David Allen. This book is all about creating a system to execute on your myriad tasks, projects and responsibilities. In plain language, he guides you through a process to ensure nothing ever gets missed and you'll meet all of those important deadlines.

The Power of Moments: Why Certain Experiences Have Extraordinary Impact by Chip Heath and Dan Heath. This book is by the authors of the better-known book *Switch: How to Change Things When Change is Hard*. I love this more recent book because the authors apply the science behind what we remember most to two very important groups: customers and employees. Filled with practical suggestions you can do today, you'll learn that businesses who create memorable experiences generate staunch loyalty among customers and employees. This book will change the way you think about the customer experience, and it will make you a better leader to those who work for you.

Strategy #2: Exude Executive Presence

You've probably heard the term executive presence. But you might not know what it is. Executive presence is an all-encompassing term describing the image a successful executive projects. When you have good executive presence, your bosses can easily envision you as a colleague. When you lack it, people will question your skills, no matter how experienced you are.

Sylvia Ann Hewlett defines executive presence as the missing link between merit and success in the subtitle of her book *Executive Presence*. If you've received feedback that you need to improve your executive presence, her book should be a priority on your reading list. Otherwise, this chapter will provide you with enough information to polish and maintain your executive image.

The sections in this chapter give two main components of executive presence: looking like a professional and minding your manners. In each section, you'll find a list of specific characteristics you must have to exhibit executive presence.

Look Like a Professional

An important part of demonstrating executive presence is looking the part. People must be able to imagine you as an executive when they are considering you for a promotion. If you don't look the part, you're going to have a hard time advancing.

Most people understand they have to dress well. But many don't understand the smaller details needed to look like an executive. Read the list below to learn the many components that contribute to an executive look.

1. Up-level clothes. Up-level means wearing the same type of clothes your boss wears. It's usually not enough to wear the nicest clothes for your current job. You should choose clothes and styling those in positions higher than you wear. Even if you have the type of job where a polo shirt and khaki pants are the norm, you can "up-level" your style by choosing nicer pants, wearing a jacket when at office meetings, and ensuring that your shoes are polished and not overly worn.

2. Boring clothes. Unless you're in the fashion industry, boring clothes are safer than flashy ones. Once you've established your brand and received the position you'd like, you can get a bit more creative. But in general, office attire means plain old boring office attire. You can add color through blouses, scarves, pocket squares and cool ties. People who choose styles that are funky and flashy risk becoming more well-known for their style than their substance. And in some office cultures, you will be frowned upon or even mocked for non-standard styles.

3. Ironed, cleaned, and mended clothes. At all times, you must demonstrate an attention to these details of your clothing. If you don't, people will assume your work ethic

and attention to detail are as messy as your clothes. When clothes aren't ironed or cleaned properly, or when buttons are missing or hems are frayed, people notice. There's nothing wrong with saving money by purchasing clothes second-hand. Just ensure that by the time you wear them, they look new. It might be unconscious, but people will judge you as not worthy of a higher-level position if your clothes look unkempt.

4. Polished and well-kept shoes. A corollary to the above, you also need to ensure your shoes match an executive look. You don't need to buy $1,000 Jimmy Choos to be an executive. You can purchase nice looking $50 (or even less) shoes at the local mall. Ensure the leather stays looking new and the heels aren't damaged or dented. Save money buying new shoes by having the heels and leather refurbished at a shoe repair store for less than $10. Your favorite shoes will come out looking like new.

5. Effective undergarments. Undergarments are no longer made just to cover your privates. They are now made to help your clothes look better. They can help you look slimmer. They smooth out any non-muscle-related lumps under your clothes. This goes for men and for women. If your clothes hang oddly on you, if your panty lines are obvious, if your underwear band creates a muffin top, you are going to look sloppy. Your bosses will assume your work is sloppy. Whatever your shape, invest in undergarments designed to keep you smoothed out. The Spanx brand is the gold standard, and they make all types of undergarments, for all needs, for men and for women. But you can find similar products at a discount if you look.

6. Un-sexy. Men typically don't have the same issues as women do with regard to clothes that may look "sexy". Call it unfair, but the reality is that women will be judged for

looking too sexy. Women should always wear a camisole if any portion of their cleavage is showing. Skirts and dresses should not hit any higher than right above the knee. If you are tall, you might have a problem finding skirts that are long enough. Go online and special order them. Or wear nice pants and a jacket instead. Also avoid lacy leggings or tights that show skin through them. If it's a hot climate, you can go without nylons, of course. But when it gets cooler out, stick to normal opaque tights. If you are a female and have any elements of a "sexy" look, people will think you are trying to leverage your looks to get a promotion. Worse yet, they may think your looks are the only reason you got a promotion.

7. Appropriate make-up. When it comes to make-up, you should approach it in terms of having an office look that can, and in most cases should, be different from your weekend or evening look. This is true whether you prefer heavy make up when going out or no makeup at all on the weekends. Ultimately, make up is your personal choice. Just know that some research has shown that women who wear heavier, but appropriately applied, makeup are actually seen as more competent. Whatever your choice, if you're a woman over the age of 30, you need to wear some. The best make-up for the office is heavy enough to cover up those wrinkles or imperfections that show more as you age. Go to any department store, tell them you need an office look, and give them your overall preferences of heavier or lighter. Then listen and do what they tell you. It's worth it to have a professional help. Once you've gotten it down, you can probably shop for cheaper makeup at your local drugstore.

8. Clothes that fit well. Whatever size you are, make sure your clothes fit well. I find that heavy people and very

thin people tend to choose clothes that hang on them. It's as if they think loose-fitting clothes will somehow hide their outside-the-norm body shape. Or maybe they just can't find clothes that fit them perfectly. Loose fitting clothes do not hide your shape. They make you look sloppy, and they detract from your executive presence. Whatever size you are, embrace it. If your shape is outside the average, you might need to have your clothes tailored to fit right, but it will be worth the investment. Also, these days you can find online stores that tailor clothes exactly to your body measurements, at a fraction of the cost of in-store tailoring.

9. Hair natural and updated. Your hair doesn't need to be your natural hair color. But it does need to be someone's natural hair color. If you want to be taken seriously in the workplace, you need to avoid extreme platinum blonde. You must be equally cautious with jet black unless it's your natural look. Never, ever add colors like purple, pink, and blue to your hair if you're looking to advance your career. If you color your hair, remember that most hair has several shades in it, so invest in highlights if you need them. In addition, keep your look updated. Don't let your roots grow out too much, and make sure your style is in fashion. If you think you might be out of date, spend the money to go to an expensive hair stylist once and tell them you want a complete update. After that, a less-expensive hair stylist can usually replicate the look going forward. If you're a balding man, never grow it out and comb it over. Avoid toupees unless they are of the highest quality and no one would guess you're wearing one. Keep the sides clean or shave your head completely to ensure you project an updated image.

10. Nails, feet, face and teeth groomed. Don't ruin your executive look with dirty or ragged nails and skin—

on your hands or your feet. You can do it yourself, but be sure to clip your nails, clean them, and keep your cuticles and heels looking moisturized. Equally important, don't let any aspect of your face distract from your look. You must eliminate any unwanted hairs—chin, eyebrows, mustache, nose. Have them waxed or trim them yourself. And finally, keep your teeth white and straight. Your smile is the first thing people see when they greet you. If it's damaged, you won't make a good impression. Unfortunately, it's very expensive to fix heavily stained or crooked teeth. But if you don't, it will hold you back from attaining higher-level positions.

In summary, probably no one will tell you that some part of your personal appearance is preventing you from advancing. That's because people are too embarrassed to say something, or they don't even know they have an unconscious bias against you. If you're not sure, ask several friends or trusted colleagues. Begin the conversations by saying, "I want to get your advice. Do you think I should (update my clothes, fix my teeth, change my hairstyle, get a manicure…)?" That is a non-threatening question to which they will likely reply with their honest opinion. If you get consistent responses to any one question, then listen. Take the steps you need to begin elevating your executive look.

Mind Your Manners

Once you look the part of an executive, you have to act the part also. This book describes many actions that will help you advance into a higher level role. But there are also actions that are simply expected of any executive. If you neglect them, your executive presence will be damaged.

THE ANTI-ENTREPRENEUR

Below I list ten manners and behaviors you should exhibit on a daily basis. Read the list to refresh the importance of these actions. Evaluate your own image, and take steps to improve if you note any area that might be lacking.

1. Say please and thank you. When anyone at work does something nice for you, thank them. Err on the side of thanking for every little thing rather than not thanking enough. When you need to make a request, say please. Use please and thank you when working with colleagues at all levels—including people who work for you.

2. Don't swear. Even if everyone around you swears, be the person who doesn't. You never know who you might be offending, because individuals are generally not going to ask you to stop. If your boss swears, you are probably safe letting loose with a cuss word every once in a while. However, if you consistently drop f-bombs at work, you will lose the respect of many coworkers. Your swearing might not be offensive to them, but it won't help them see you as an executive, either.

3. Use good grammar and spelling. Few speech patterns hurt you more than poor grammar. If English is your second language, people tend to be more understanding when you make a verbal grammatical error. But when you send a business email, people expect you to have proofed it in advance. If you need to brush up on your grammar, take one of the free online courses available via the "massive open online curriculum" (MOOC) options many major universities offer.

4. Enunciate your words. You must always fully enunciate your words. Don't drop consonants and blend words. For example, don't say "Do-ya wanna go-ta lunch?" Instead, say, "Do you want to go to lunch?" If

English is your second language, or if you grew up in a culture where English was very casual, make it a priority to practice accurate word pronunciation. Having an accent isn't problematic at all. Having an accent no one can understand is a big problem. The easiest way to exhibit better pronunciation is to slow down your speech. Also ask friends to critique you after a conversation or public speaking engagement.

5. Be confident. You might think that confidence comes from within. For the most part, you're right. But did you know you can trick your brain into thinking you are confident? If your brain thinks it, you will project it. Executive presence always shines when you exude confidence. According to research in the book *Presence* by Amy Cuddy (referenced earlier), you need to keep your posture and stance as open as possible. Google "power poses" to see images of stances that will convince your brain you're more confident than you feel.

6. Eat smart. Worry less about nutritional value and more about making a good impression. When you go out to eat with work colleagues, don't talk while chewing. And by all means don't order the tacos, the french dip, the messy pizza, or anything else you have to eat with your hands. Instead, choose an entree that won't have you licking your fingers and dripping sauce on your shirt.

7. Maintain a positive outlook. Nobody likes a negative nelly. In large groups and in small groups, be the person who sees the upside of situations. It's fine to be authentic if something really needs to change, but always offer a solution after a complaint. If you are negative, people will see you as someone who is unable to resolve problems. And if you can't generate good solutions, you can't be an effective executive.

8. Be friendly. Being nice to people helps your brand. You don't need to be mean to be an executive—in fact you will probably be looked down upon if you are. Instead, be nice to everyone you meet. Smile at them. Ask about their day. Listen to what they say. Especially in large companies, managers move departments and locations frequently. You never know when the person you meet will be in a position to say, "I really like him, he's really friendly" to a potential hiring manager.

9. Don't interrupt. Interrupting others before they are done speaking is rude. In addition, if you're already thinking about what you want to say before your colleague is done speaking, then you're not listening very well. Wait until the person talking is finished. Don't just wait for a pause so you can insert your opinion before anyone else. If you do accidentally interrupt, say "I'm sorry" and stop talking. As I explain fully in the next chapter, you will always look better if you focus more on listening than on talking.

10. Change your mind. During your career, you're going to express opinions others disagree with. And others will say things you believe are inaccurate or uninformed. In work debates, you must let others influence your thinking. If you never change your mind, you'll be seen as an arrogant know-it-all. Plus you won't learn as much as you should, and no one will want to work with you.

Strategy #3: Be Trustworthy

Being trustworthy is one of the most advantageous characteristics to be known for. Because of that, it's not a perception you can leave to chance. You must take active steps to show people that they can trust you. When they do so, you'll receive four very important benefits that will help your opportunities for promotion:

1. You'll have access to information about your company that others don't have. If you are trustworthy, your boss and other leaders are more likely to share information with you. You will find yourself in the know about company initiatives long before others are made aware. If you know about upcoming mergers, acquisitions, major projects or personnel changes, you can prepare yourself for them in advance. You can strategically seek out work assignments that will put you in a good position to stand out among your peers.

2. You'll have access to information about other leaders and people. When your colleagues trust you, they are more likely to share information about their perceptions of other workers and leaders in the organization. This is important because it gives you a better idea about who is respected, who is likely to be promoted, and who to avoid. That

information can help you choose a mentor or decide which opinion to listen to the most in a meeting. Of course you will get along with everyone, but knowing how well others are respected (or not), will help you pay attention to the right leaders and avoid political land mines.

3. You will be seen as smarter and wiser. The opposite of being trustworthy is being indiscriminate about what you say. When you share information you've received from others, even if it's relatively unimportant, you will be seen as lacking discretion and judgment. Your colleagues will wonder "If he's telling me X about what Bob told him, he might be telling Bob what I tell him about Y." On the flip side, when you listen to information but don't share it, you'll be seen as smarter and wiser. You'll be able to act without others knowing your motivation, and when your decisions turn out well, they will see you as smarter.

4. You will be given important assignments. When your boss and coworkers know you can be trusted to follow through on your commitments in a timely manner, it's more likely you'll be assigned high-profile projects. They will rely upon you as the person who can complete assignments on time, with confidentiality. Being the point person for high-profile projects will help you get noticed by senior leaders who decide on promotional opportunities.

10 Ways to Develop Trust

Here are ten concrete strategies that will help you develop trust at work:

1. Follow through. At work, you have to take care of work issues ranging from sending an email to developing a project plan to setting up a meeting. Whatever you commit to do, follow through without others needing to remind you.

If you find yourself making commitments while rushing from one meeting to the next, find a good strategy for tracking commitments so you don't forget. Always bring a piece of paper to write on, send yourself texts or emails, or use a popular note-taking or "to-do" tracking application on your phone or tablet.

2. Help others without taking credit. In large organizations, everyone, understandably, wants to stand out among their peers. Once a group project is finished, all contributors want to get their individual credit. Even when helping another individual, workers want to be acknowledged in some way. This is a natural desire. However, if you openly seek credit for your work, you'll look arrogant and selfish. Have faith that over time, if you help enough people, you will develop the perception that your help comes for free. This will engender informal support for your endeavors. You might not be openly acknowledged as much as the person seeking credit, but you will be better liked and more positively spoken of. That said, the one person you should tell when you spend time helping others is your own boss. Your boss can help speak positively about you; this third party advocacy will go much further than you grabbing credit for yourself. Your peers will seek you out because they trust that you will help them without turning it into a career-advancement headline.

3. Give others credit. This is a corollary to the concept of helping others without taking credit. Whether it's your boss, your colleagues, or your own employees, always give someone else credit. Rest assured that most people will know and understand what your contributions have been. When you give credit to others for their contributions, you develop trust. Others will want you on their team because they know you will make them look good. The more projects

and initiatives you're on, the better your own career brand. The more you give others credit, the more you develop the perception that you are an effective collaborator.

4. Only say what you know to be true. When you are talking to others, only give factual information. This will ensure that when you say something, people can trust it's true. Don't speculate on what others have said, and never share information that may not be true. This advice applies to information about other people, the company, data, or reports. Be aware that others might say the information they are sharing is true, just to make themselves look "in the know." Don't fall for it. Independently verify the information before you pass it along. Make it a habit to only provide neutral or positive information to others. Finally, even if you know negative information is true, you don't need to share it unless it's information your boss needs.

5. Never say who you received information from. Unless information is completely neutral, don't share who you heard it from. You'll get more information if people trust that when they tell you something, you're not going to blab about them blabbing. Having access to information will help you plan helpful pathways throughout your career. When your coworkers trust you won't give up your source, they will be more likely to continue giving you information.

6. Be confidential. Related to the above, when someone asks you not to share a piece of information, honor their request. No one is going to seek you out for help if they think you're going to tell others about the conversation. Don't even imply that you know information. Remain silent. If someone asks you directly about a piece of confidential information, just end the conversation. Say, "I'm sure we'll all know more about it when or if the time is right." Eventually people will trust you more because

when they find out you actually did know, they will realize you kept it totally confidential. And then they'll share their secrets with you.

7. Don't trust your most trustworthy friends. This is a hard one, especially if you work with one of your very best friends. Nevertheless, you must keep confidential information away from even these best friends. Yes, I know you trust them. However, this is how it works. You tell your ONE most trustworthy friend a juicy piece of information. Then he tells his other ONE most trustworthy friend. And he tells his, and so on. After a week, everyone knows. In addition, you might tell your friend something that he believes he has a professional obligation to tell to his boss. Protect yourself and your friends from difficult situations by not sharing confidential information. In the long run, it will help both you and your friend. And it will ensure that others in your organization can trust that the two of you aren't sharing secrets.

8. Share wisdom and technical knowledge. The type of information you should share to develop trust is your own wisdom, advice and technical knowledge, when asked. As you become more experienced in your role, others are likely to ask you for advice. They might come to you for mentoring. They might ask you to explain a particularly difficult concept. Always agree to share your knowledge. When you do so, people trust you as a seasoned professional. You will develop a reputation for helping others to grow. In turn, the people you help will be loyal to you.

9. Be the shepherd, not the flock. This is a phrase from leadership expert John Maxwell. It can apply to having original ideas, but it also applies to developing trust. If everyone is talking about a specific piece of information or gossip, be the voice of reason. Maybe everyone has

heard of an impending takeover and is panicked. You will develop trust if you can stay calm, offering an alternative to "the sky is falling" thinking. When groups of people are flipping out over a new development, think about the opposite viewpoint. Then, either stay silent, which shows your calm nature, or offer an alternate opinion, which shows your balance. Both approaches will help people see you as a leader who can be trusted to demonstrate calm in a storm.

10. Be open and approachable. It helps you connect with others if people see you as a real person. Sharing your passion, your opinions and even your small mistakes can help you develop relationships with others. When your coworkers and employees see you as a "real" person, they are more likely to trust you. When they realize that your life isn't perfect, that you make mistakes too, they will be more inclined to share their own thoughts and fears. However, you have to walk a fine line between being open with your thoughts and sharing too much. In the next section, I list ten things you should never share with coworkers.

What Not to Share About Yourself

Disclosing information about yourself can help make you more approachable. But to be trustworthy, you must avoid disclosing facts that will hurt your personal brand and your reputation. Think of the people you trust at work. What do they share with others about their personal lives? Most likely, the information they share is limited to positive anecdotes and observations.

Sure, everyone makes mistakes. And most people have suffered through humiliations, indiscretions, and setbacks of some kind. That doesn't mean you need to share them with your coworkers in order to connect. Connecting to develop trust is about finding commonalities. It's not about disclosing information that makes you look lacking in judgment.

Here are some topics you should never share about yourself. Keep these, and any related topics, out of your work discussions.

1. Your sex life, even if you're married.
2. How much you hate a member of your family.
3. How much you hate a co-worker.
4. How drunk you got last weekend.
5. How much you relax when you smoke pot (even if it's legal).
6. The fact that you cheated on your spouse, or that your spouse cheated on you.
7. Your therapy sessions.
8. Your Xanax or other anti-anxiety prescription.
9. Your misconduct termination from a previous job.
10. Who you had a one-night stand with at your last work conference.
11. The fact that your spouse never supports you emotionally.
12. Your bankruptcy.
13. Your retirement date.
14. Your interview with another company.
15. Your fake sick call when you went camping.

Listen More Than Talk

Listening more than talking also helps develop trust, and it gives you several other advantages. It allows you to observe how a conversation is going before you interject an opinion. You can see how various people react, or what their arguments are, which may change your approach. And in general, when you talk less, you influence more. Your colleagues will trust that you have thoughtfully considered their opinions and ideas.

Imagine it this way. Let's say you have one main concept you want people to understand. It's strategic, insightful, and smart. If you bury it in a rainfall of less important remarks, your most impressive comment is likely to be missed.

Another reason listening helps develop trust is that it builds rapport with others. People feel a connection when they are listened to. They feel as if their thoughts are valued. Others will respect and like you only if you demonstrate that you respect and like them in return. You do this through active, thoughtful listening.

Even when trying to break the speaking habit, most people don't know how to listen effectively. There are specific behaviors, however, that will help you do so. At your next meeting, use the ten strategies I've provided in this section. Your actions will demonstrate that you are listening and that you appreciate others' comments as well.

1. Rarely be the first person to speak. Unless specifically asked to start the conversation, let someone else go first. If you must go first, ask a question rather than making a proclamation. Waiting to speak allows you to understand what others are thinking before you jump in with your opinion.

2. Count before speaking again. If you like to talk a lot, you probably love meetings where you get to offer your opinion. You may see discussions as an opportunity to "impress the boss" or wow your colleagues with your in-depth understanding of the issues. Your boss will be impressed by your results, not by your ability to dominate

a conversation. To break the habit, count speakers before you speak again. Count to the number in the room and divide it in half. For example, if there are fourteen people in the discussion, let seven other people talk before you talk again. Seven different people don't need to talk, but there must be at least seven other comments before you speak again.

3. Ask two questions first. Most people are so anxious to get their opinion heard that they don't truly listen to others' viewpoints. The best way to break yourself of that habit, and to connect with others, is to ask at least two questions before you offer your opinion. When you force yourself to ask questions, you force yourself to really listen first. That helps you make a more informed statement when you do choose to share your opinion.

4. Hear their story before defending yours. It is common in the workplace to present an idea to a group and get feedback. Before you begin to defend your own ideas, listen carefully to everything your colleagues have to say. Ask questions to elicit others' reasons for their opinions. You need not always agree, but if you give the appearance you're not even listening to others' stories, no one will want to work with you.

5. Use positive non-verbals. Simply asking insightful questions is a huge step in the right direction. Ensuring that your non-verbal communication matches what you are saying is also critical. When listening, exhibit open body language. Nod to the person giving feedback. Take a few notes. Smile when appropriate to show you like others' contributions to the discussion. These behaviors have the added benefit of reminding your brain that you are listening, which keeps it from thinking about your next verbal response.

6. Proactively ask for others' opinions. Multiple research studies demonstrate that people will feel more connected to you when you ask for their advice. That said, saying, "I'd like to get your opinion" won't have any impact if people think you're just doing it for a political reason. Be very specific regarding why that person's opinion matters. For example, you could say, "I'd like to get your opinion because I know you have more expertise in ____ area than I do." You can follow up with, "Oh that's great, could you tell me more about…?" This will encourage the person to talk more, allowing you to demonstrate you are listening.

7. No matter how right you think you are, consider you might be wrong. Enter every conversation with the idea that your beliefs going in are likely to be altered. In fact, when you truly listen to others, their thoughts and ideas should alter yours. When you allow that to happen, others will feel listened to. And your own ideas will become better. Always remember that your way of approaching the situation might not be the best. Your knowledge might be right in one context, but not a fit for the current one. Even if you don't respect or like the person giving an alternative opinion, consider that some portion of their viewpoint could be right.

8. Don't be the loudest voice in the room — literally. Some of us are naturally loud speakers. We are animated, we use our hands, and we are passionate with our opinions. That's not terrible, but when the volume of your voice rises above everyone else's, you will inhibit others' ability to listen. You will also inhibit others' desire to share their own opinions. Frequently, when you are the loudest voice in the room, you will be the only person talking because no one else wants to attempt to match your volume. Moderate the tone of your voice to match others who are speaking. In

addition, when you vary your volume from louder to softer, people will pay more attention to your words.

9. Don't be the smartest person in the room. The higher you move up in the organization, the easier it is to have the most knowledge, the most history, the most opinions on a variety of topics. Similarly, when your education level is higher than the people you're interacting with, you'll be tempted to share that knowledge, especially when you just know you're right. No one feels listened to if they feel they are getting a professorial lecture. Resist the urge to bless others with your font of knowledge. Instead, listen to your colleagues' ideas and build off of them. You can use your knowledge to make good decisions, but you don't need to tell others you're doing so. Every time you feel the urge to quote the latest research or rely on your vast and diverse experiences, ask a question instead.

10. Acknowledge others' comments equally. Many times we only acknowledge the comments of those we agree with. Worse yet, we have a tendency to more readily accept opinions from those who look like us or who have similar backgrounds. It will become apparent if you selectively acknowledge others' opinions. Make sure comments such as, "That's a good point" and "Thank you for that feedback" are distributed equally among all your colleagues. This will ensure that all the people you interact with feel listened to and valued.

Strategy #4: Choose the Right Boss

You won't always have the luxury of choosing the right boss. But when you do, choose wisely. An important factor to consider when seeking any promotion is who you're going to work for. Choose poorly, and your options for advancement could stagnate. Choose wisely, and your options for advancement will grow and accelerate. The next section provides ten factors to consider when you have a choice about who your boss is going to be. The sections that follow describe how to handle a difficult boss, and how to leave a really bad one.

10 Characteristics of the Right Boss

Your future boss should have as many characteristics below as possible. You'll see that the qualities range from the very practical to the somewhat subjective. Rate your potential boss using a scale of 1 (low) through 10 (high) in each of the ten areas. Anything less than a score of 50, and you might want to reconsider that job opportunity. If you have the choice between two different opportunities with two different bosses, choose the boss who rated the highest.

1. Respected. You want your boss to be a respected member of the organization. Your boss is in a position to advocate for your career advancement. If nobody listens, it won't help you. On the flip side, having a boss who isn't respected by his colleagues could damage your own brand. You might be the best employee in the world, but if no one in your organization respects your boss, others might think you're just like him. In addition, complete respect typically comes with time. Think twice if the boss hiring you is very new in the organization, and you would be too. You could find yourself being pushed out as well if the boss who hired you isn't successful.

2. Connected. Having a well-connected boss expands your own professional network. You will be introduced to key leaders who can help you advance your career. You will be put in social situations that allow you to develop relationships with others outside your organization. As I describe in a later chapter, developing a networking web is critical not only to help you get a promotion, but to guard against remaining unemployed if you have been laid off.

3. Promotable. It's important that your boss is promotable. If he's not, then your opportunity to move into his position is zero. If having your boss's position isn't your focus, you still benefit having a promotable boss. If your boss moves into a higher-level position, he might hire you to work for him in that new role. At a minimum, working in a new department or location will garner you more professional exposure. Better yet, following your boss to his new role might even be a promotion, or more money, for you.

4. Mobile. Ideally, you want your boss to have geographic mobility. This opens up his own options for promotion if they aren't available in your organization.

When your boss is place bound, there are fewer options to move up, especially if your boss is already at or near the top of your org chart. If your boss moves, you may have an opportunity to get his job. And if your boss moves to a new location, you'll have a connection in another area if you need a job later in your career.

5. Loyal. Having a boss who is loyal to you is critical. Loyalty comes in different forms. Your boss should stick up for you when you make a mistake. Your boss should speak highly of you to others. If your boss gives you constructive criticism, it should be in private. In short, your boss should be the type who praises publicly and criticizes privately. If your boss tells everyone else about your professional weaknesses, it will damage your brand, regardless of what he actually thinks of your potential. It should be a huge red flag for you if you hear your potential boss criticizing his employees to others.

6. Supportive. You want your boss to be supportive of your growth. This means he will take the time to teach and mentor you. It's not helpful to your learning if your boss gives you a challenging assignment and never talks to you about it until you're done. You want the type of boss who will guide your work until you have achieved mastery. And once you get really good at one responsibility, your boss should give you another stretch assignment to continue your learning. If you see your potential boss's employees getting promotions, you can assume he's investing in their development. If you see large numbers of employees who work for your potential boss quitting or getting fired, you can assume he's not a good people-developer.

7. Trustworthy. You need to trust that when your boss tells you something, it's accurate. You need to trust that when you confide in your boss, he's not telling anyone else.

And you need to trust that your boss isn't telling you what a great job you do while at the same time agreeing with your critics that you need to do better. If your potential boss is known for sharing sensitive information, you can guess he'll share things about you also. Want to see how trustworthy your potential boss is? Ask him point-blank what gaps or areas of development he sees for one of his current direct reports. If you don't even work for him yet and he's willing to talk about others' growth areas, walk away.

8. Ethical. You do not want to be put in a position of having to cover for the sins of your boss. First, it could make you complicit in his escapades. Second, your boss could expect you to "join in" to some extent. If you don't, and his other employees do, then you might find yourself on the outs. You will most likely know in advance if your potential boss is prone to morally questionable activities. Over-drinking, sexual promiscuity, making questionable business decisions, and adultery are usually hot topics of office gossip. You can't rely on one rumor to judge your potential boss, but if the talk is consistent, ongoing, and pervasive, then stay away. Only work for bosses who have a reputation for high ethical standards.

9. Responsible. You want your boss to be a responsible hard-worker. You don't want a boss who misses deadlines and delays important projects. And you certainly don't want a boss who will blame you or call you to work on a Sunday because of his poor planning. That said, be careful that your boss isn't a workaholic. Unless you're willing to work 12-hour days yourself, you want a boss who has a good work-life balance. That way, you will also be able to maintain a reasonable work schedule.

10. Close to retirement-eligible. This is an important consideration if you aspire to get your boss's job when

he leaves. Note however that I say "close" to retirement eligible. You don't want a boss who hires you and then leaves shortly thereafter. If you've chosen your boss wisely, you need to have enough time to learn from him before he retires. Even if you aren't hired to replace him, a boss who is loyal to you and retires will ensure that your company respects you enough to foster your future career opportunities. On the other hand, if your boss plans to stay in his job forever, it may impact your ability to move up. This will be especially true if your boss's job is the only position in your organization in your upward career path.

Not all of these ten factors will be equally important to you. However, ranking all of them will give you a fairly objective way of evaluating if any potential boss will help, or hinder, your career advancement.

How to Handle a Difficult Boss

Throughout your career, you'll probably have many bosses. If you've been able to choose the right boss most of the time, count yourself lucky. But you won't get it right 100% of the time. Sometimes this is because your ego—and your desire for a promotion with more money—lead you to taking a job with a boss no one else wants to work for. Sometimes you were hired by a great boss who leaves and is replaced by a bad one.

No matter the circumstances, expect that at some point you'll encounter a boss who is less than helpful to your career. You may even encounter one you intensely dislike. Sometimes your boss is a good boss to other people, but just not a match for you personally. Sometimes your boss is highly respected by upper management, and yet you see all of his true flaws.

As soon as you realize you have a bad boss, you need to begin planning your eventual exit. But before you can leave, you need tangible strategies to survive. You probably won't have the luxury of switching jobs right away. Thus, the strategies below explain how to handle your difficult boss while working in that job. The section after that gives you advice for how to handle your departure. Follow the advice in both sections to ensure that you extricate yourself from a bad leader with your career aspirations in tact.

1. Plan your strategies in advance. Know the coping mechanisms available to you ahead of time. This will help you avoid acting out of emotion in the heat of the moment, which will only damage your future career options. If necessary, post positive reminders on your mirror so you'll see them each morning before going to work.

2. Focus on what you are learning. You can learn just as much from a bad boss as you can a good one. Pay attention to what your boss is doing wrong. Make yourself analyze why the strategy isn't working. Think about what you would do better. In addition, ask your boss about his strategy behind certain processes or decisions. You might not agree with him, but at least you'll have a better understanding of his thought process.

3. Consider the fact your perception may be wrong. It's important to consider that your boss may have traits that make him a good boss in ways your company wants. Perhaps he's just not a good boss for your particular style or work preferences. Some leaders are brought into an organization for the specific purpose of taking care of problems left by a predecessor. They are hired to shake things up. Behavior that might seem mean, challenging, or overly critical may be exactly what your company hired your boss to do. Consider your situation carefully. Are

you one of the people your boss was brought in to "fix" or "change"? If so, you will need to align yourself with your boss right away, or switch jobs.

4. Examine your own flaws. It's commonly known that we most vehemently criticize traits we also see in ourselves. For example, you might complain that your boss is disorganized and makes last minute decisions. Yet you might have gotten that same criticism in the past. Or maybe you secretly judge yourself for having those same tendencies. Consider also that you're not perfect. Some bosses are so good that they help us overcome our flaws. It might be that you think your boss is bad because his shortcomings only amplify your own.

5. Fake it till you make it. Research tells us that if we fake smiling, our brains begin to believe we're happier. The same is true when you have a bad boss. Rather than going in to work every day thinking, "I can't believe I have to deal with this asshole," change your mindset. Start faking that you like your boss. How would you behave? What would you do? Chances are that if you dislike your boss, your boss senses it. Change that dynamic by acting as if your boss is the best one you've ever had. An added benefit is that your boss is likely to treat you better if he believes you really like and respect him.

6. Avoid giving feedback directly to your boss. If you have a good relationship with your boss, and if your position level is close to his, it's safe to offer him advice or constructive help. But when you have a bad relationship with your boss, I highly recommend you do not. Generally speaking, no one listens to criticism from people they don't like or respect. If your boss has demonstrated an open dislike for you, or if your boss is demonstrably unethical, there is no reason to give him feedback. If you do, he might

tell you to your face that he appreciates the feedback, but you cannot trust he won't use it against you later. Worse, as I've seen happen in other situations, he could accuse you of complaining just because you don't have enough to do in your own job.

7. Do give feedback if asked directly by human resources, an executive coach, or your boss's boss. If asked for feedback about your boss from your regular colleagues, don't give it. Remain confidential and positive. But if asked by influential people in the organization, you must give it. This is because if these people are asking you, they are looking for ways your boss could, or should, improve. It doesn't mean your boss is being fired, so you must be strategic about how you provide the feedback. But it does mean someone has noticed that your boss could improve in order to be a better leader. You will help your own situation if you give suggestions and feedback when asked to do so by the appropriate person in your organization.

7. Remind yourself it's temporary. It's rare that you have to put up with a bad boss for your entire career. You will come and go from departments and organizations, and your bosses will come and go as well. The situation can be as temporary as you make it. If you choose to look for another job, it might take a while to find one, but eventually, you will. You always have the choice to leave, and thus, by definition your situation is temporary.

8. Document unethical behavior. If you have a boss who breaks laws, commits harassment or discrimination, or lies to his employer, you must document the behavior. There are several reasons to do so. First, you want to protect yourself by having evidence if someone wants to blame you. Second, you want to protect yourself by having evidence of your boss's behavior if he tries to fire you. Third, if you

are ever called upon to testify in a legal proceeding, you'll be surprised at how much you might forget if you don't document it along the way. Finally, when you document events as they occur, your perception of what occurred will generally be considered more reliable than if you try to remember details later on. You need not tell anyone you are documenting events. You may never even need to use your documentation. But you do need to keep it for unforeseen circumstances.

9. Do everything possible to make a personal connection with your boss. Even if your boss makes your life miserable, continue to attempt making a personal connection with him. Take him to lunch or breakfast. Ask him about his family or kids. Wish him good luck on important presentations. Remember his birthday. Making small but kind gestures toward your boss could help pave the way for a more authentic connection. This could in turn help you work with him more productively. Eventually, you might be able to problem-solve ways he can reduce the bad behavior that impacts you.

10. Plan your exit before getting fired. As soon as you realize your relationship with your boss won't improve, you need to begin planning your exit. Don't go down fighting to the bitter end, hoping to see your boss's demise. In most disagreements between bosses and their subordinates, the boss wins. There is also no reason for you to go into work stressed everyday, wondering if you're going to be fired. It's always easier to find a job when you have a job. Thus, even if you have to take a small pay cut, it is safest to secure a new position far away from the boss you dislike.

How to Leave a Bad Boss

When you leave a bad boss, you'll probably want to get in a few good digs at him as you leave. Maybe you want to write a scathing letter about how horrible he was and send it to his boss. Maybe you want to initiate a complaint conversation with human resources. These are terrible ideas.

You don't know what your boss has told others about you. Your complaints might seem overly critical, so you'll risk alienating the entire organization on your way out. You don't want to make more enemies besides your boss.

If you're in the same line of work, it doesn't behoove you to piss off human resources or your boss's boss. Keep a good relationship with everyone involved. Others who love your boss might know someone in your new organization. You could be characterized as a problem-maker to your new employer. Also, by taking the high road, when your boss finally leaves the organization, you might have an opportunity to return.

In that context, here are some key strategies to ensure your departure is viewed as a normal transition. It's always better for people to think you had a positive reason for leaving instead of an ongoing conflict with your boss.

1. Find a natural time to exit. If you can, choose a logical time to leave, one that everyone will understand. My mentor Barb Wright used to call this the "moment in time." Many professions have logical moments when individuals typically transition jobs. Choose one of those time periods. Depending on your profession, it could be at the end of the school year, right after an extended holiday or vacation, when a major initiative is complete, at the end of your employment contract, on your 60th birthday, or

as your child transitions to a new school, such as middle school to high school. Unless you're getting an obvious promotion, it's not helpful to your future career options if you leave under questionable conditions in the middle of a big project, during your employment contract, or (for school leaders) in the middle of the school year. Leaving at a logical moment in time adds to the perception that you made the decision to leave rather than being forced out by a bad boss.

2. Keep your job search confidential, if possible. As you are looking for another job, keep the search confidential if you can. In private sector industries, job searches are generally confidential. Background checks rarely require a phone call to your current employer. In the public sector, job searches are usually more difficult to keep confidential due to various legal requirements of some positions. Apart from that, there is no need to tell anyone—even your closest colleagues—that you are looking for another job. Your boss could find out, and if he's truly terrible, he could start bad-mouthing you to colleagues at other organizations. That won't help you to leave the nasty boss situation you're in.

3. Share an alternate reason for switching jobs. When the time comes to tell your boss or others you're switching jobs, don't tell people it's because your boss is terrible. Instead, share an alternate reason. This will ensure that you don't burn bridges on your way out by trashing a leader others may think is effective. Try to make the reason logical and as specific as possible. The better the reason, the more likely people are to believe it. If you can't think of a reason that applies to your specific situation, a common one is, "The new job will expand my skills and provide me with more opportunities for advancement."

4. Make sure your friends and family tell the same

story. Whatever story you tell must be the same story your friends and family share. It's not going to do you any good to develop a great reason for leaving if your friends are telling everyone else that the real reason is your terrible boss. I recommend that you limit truth-telling to your spouse and your immediate family only. Even so, remind them that to everyone else, your bad boss should not be mentioned. Instead, tell them to say, "In fact, Bob really learned a lot from Mr. Boss, and considers his time a truly valuable experience." This will provide added positivity to any statement they share, even if questioned directly about the bad boss.

5. Don't criticize your boss. Even after you've left the organization, don't talk poorly about your boss. You just don't know who might know your boss and tell him. You also don't know how you will be perceived. Your new organization may begin to wonder if you were the problem, especially if you are struggling with the transition to your new role. Remaining positive and upbeat will ensure your new employer doesn't doubt your value to your previous organization.

6. Don't talk bad about your former employer in general. Even if you hold them responsible for never dealing with your bad boss, don't say negative things about your time there. The last thing you want is to burn so many bridges on your way out that you'll never have the option to work there again.

7. Find good things to say on your way out. The flip side of not saying negative things is to find positive comments that you can tell others. If others suspect the real reason is your terrible boss, show them it wasn't. Even if they too hate your boss, show them that you were making the best of the situation by continuing to learn. Find authentically

good attributes or skills your boss has. For example, if your boss never took input and believed he was always the smartest person in the room, you could say, "He was very strong in his convictions. I learned a lot from observing his confidence level even in difficult situations."

8. Be strategically honest in your exit interview. Even if the human resources department where you work initiates and conducts formal exit interviews, you need to be strategic about how you present your boss's flaws. Be sure to share your boss's positive attributes. For example, if your boss continually criticized your work after not giving you any direction to begin with, you can say, "Mr. Boss was a perfectionist, and had a strong viewpoint about how things should be done. I think this is why he was so critical of our projects. If he had given more guidance along the way, it would have helped improve the end result." In this constructive way, you can certainly share some areas that you believe your boss might improve. But do not tell anyone that your boss is the sole reason you left. Those who also hate your boss might consider you to be a traitor for bailing out. Those who love your boss will speak poorly of your behavior while exiting.

Strategy #5: Think Like Your Boss

The best way to become a boss is to think and act like one. Most people focus their thoughts on themselves. They worry about how others regard them. They worry about looking good. They worry about getting the credit they deserve.

Being attentive to your end goal, and the actions needed to get you there, is a helpful strategy. But the best strategy for success is to focus on how your boss thinks, what your boss worries about, and how you can help your boss's success. When you help your boss succeed, you help yourself get promoted. This chapter takes you into the mind of your boss so you can determine how best to help him or her.

How Does Your Boss Think?

All leaders of people are called upon to think in ways they didn't have to when they were an individual contributor. As you move up the organization, you advance from supervising yourself to managing others. Eventually you might begin managing other managers.

Leaders have varying skill levels. Your boss is somewhere on that continuum. Regardless of skill, realize that in most ways your boss is required, simply by virtue of his/her role, to look differently at the organization's needs than you do.

Approach each situation you encounter in a way that is aligned to your boss's thinking. Imagine yourself as your boss. Try to deduce how you boss's thinking might be different from yours.

Here are seven ways of thinking you need to consider when interpreting your boss's needs. For each mindset, I've suggested ways you can support your boss by adapting your own thinking.

1. Your boss must think strategically. Your boss can't just worry about the next hour or the next day. He can't just focus on one cog in the wheel. Your boss must be thinking of the big picture. Your boss thinks about the right actions that will move a strategy forward, that will propel his department or division into the future.

Your role: When talking to your boss about a problem, show that you've used strategic thinking to analyze all possible impacts of your solution. Don't present a process or a solution without explicitly listing the big picture thinking that went into your plan.

2. Your boss must think technically. You boss must be a master at the technical aspects of the job. In other words, your boss must have practical content knowledge to guide his strategic thinking. Sometimes bosses are hired for their leadership skills without having technical knowledge about the job itself. If your boss isn't a technical master, he will want someone who is. And usually, he will want to learn.

Your role: If your boss is a technical master, be sure to increase your own skills through workshops, training, and reading so that you can hold your own with him in a discussion. Your boss may find it a time suck to get you up to speed, so take initiative and do it yourself. If your boss isn't a technical master, be the person who helps him learn what he needs to know when the time is right. But also, be that technical master he can trust to take care of the technical details behind the scenes.

3. Your boss must think empathetically. Not all bosses are good at this, but nevertheless it's an important concept for you to master. Your boss must be able to demonstrate empathy for employees in difficult situations. Even if someone is being fired for misconduct, a good boss will always think about the person, not the behavior, and will respond accordingly. When your boss thinks empathetically, employees are more engaged. On a practical level, employees are less likely to file complaints, grievances, or lawsuits when they feel their boss sees them as a real person and demonstrates empathy for their situation.

Your role: Regardless of your boss's skillset in this area, you will always help your boss by treating your coworkers with empathy. And if your boss is great at demonstrating empathy, show that you understand and agree with his approach. Avoid creating conflict by wondering out loud why on earth your boss was so nice to that incompetent, mean SOB in the office next door. If your boss isn't naturally empathetic, be his go-to person helping keep all of your coworkers engaged. Send cards that your boss signs. Offer to send flowers on behalf of your boss. Overall, help your boss recognize your co-workers' birthdays, graduations, funerals, divorces, and other major life events.

4. Your boss must think relationally. Your boss has to think about his relationships with peers. He has to network with others in ways that will help him achieve his own goals. In any organization, developing and maintaining positive relationships is critical. Thinking relationally helps

your boss get his work done in an efficient manner. When things go wrong, your boss can leverage those established relationships to backtrack and regroup. People are more likely to give others "a break" when they like the person they are working with.

Your role: Help your boss by developing and maintaining your own professional relationships. As an extension of your boss, you can use your own positive relationships to help your boss achieve his goals. If you're that lone wolf everyone hates to work with, you only create problems for your boss.

5. Your boss must think politically. Your boss must think about the political impact of his actions. Fail to do so, and he could find himself on the outs with those who have the power to help his career. For example, your boss might have a fabulous idea to change a process and make it more efficient. But maybe that process is in a different department. Your boss needs to think about how that department's leader will feel about the change. Or maybe your boss's boss has made a terrible decision, one your boss knows is bad for the organization. Your boss needs to think about how to approach it in a way that won't hurt his career. Your boss may even decide, in both situations, that the best decision is ultimately to do nothing.

Your role: The most important way you can help your boss think politically is to support those decisions made for political reasons, rather than question them. You might be frustrated your boss didn't speak up to oppose a decision when he should have. But you need to show him you recognize that among several options, one choice is always to do nothing at all. If you are aware of political mistakes your boss has made in the past, you can help him prevent future ones. Try offering alternative pathways. You might say, "That's a great idea, and you are totally right. But I think if we waited a little while until John left, you'd get more traction on your proposal." Ultimately, your boss will decide what he thinks is best. Show him your support by demonstrating you understand the political ramifications of his decision-making.

6. Your boss must think efficiently. Your boss has limited time. He typically has several employees who report directly to him, and you're just one. Even if you are your boss's only direct report, it's likely your boss has a number of goals and initiatives he is working on. Your boss usually doesn't have time for your lengthy descriptions and stories about a decision you made or an outcome you received. Also, your boss doesn't have time to make small decisions for you that you should be making yourself.

Your role: When you have a meeting with your boss, come prepared with an agenda. Arrange it so that you get your boss's most important feedback first. Summarize your main points into one or two, and then ask for a decision. If your boss needs more information to make the decision, he will tell you. In addition, have a clear understanding regarding the decisions your boss doesn't need to make for you. This will help focus your time with your boss on the items you must get input about. If you're unsure if a topic falls into the independent decision category, ask. Over time, you'll get a better sense of the decisions your boss wants you to make on your own.

7. Your boss must think holistically. Always remember that your boss has more information about large strategic initiatives than you do. Probably, he also understands the dynamics of senior leadership better than you do. That is the nature of being "higher-up" in any organization. This means that your boss is likely to see more connections

among tasks or decisions than you are. What may seem like something small to you might have greater repercussions than you know.

Your role: Although you should always plan for an efficient agenda when you meet with your boss, you need to have all of your back-up information with you. Let your boss guide the discussion to talk about what's most important to him. He will ask you to go more in-depth if he feels you're making a decision that has larger impacts. Also, do any preparation work in advance of meeting with your boss. Don't wait for your boss to say, "Did you get accounting's opinion about this?" if you know that accounting is involved. Be proactive about anticipating your boss's needs and questions in advance of meeting with him.

Now that you've learned the ways in which your boss thinks, the next section will go into depth regarding the issues your boss is likely to be worried about.

What Does Your Boss Worry About?

It will be easier to learn how to think like your boss if you also know what your boss worries about. Once you know what your boss worries about, you can take steps to help him or her.

You can be proactive with your own time, lessening the worries for your boss. You can take actions that remove the worries altogether. At the very least, you can provide an understanding ear when your boss needs a confidant.

Here is a list of items your boss likely worries about. You can assume that the more tenured your boss is in that specific role and organization, the less likely he is to worry about these issues. Nevertheless, know that at some level, even a

CEO will likely exhibit concern about many of the items on the list. As I did in the last section, for each item I've shared how you can help lessen that worry for your boss.

Your boss worries about:

1. His boss. Your boss wants his own boss to think highly of him. This is true if his boss is one person or if his "boss" is a group of trustees, board directors, or elected officials.

Your role: The best way you can help your boss in this area is to ensure your boss always looks good in front of his boss. Don't make the mistake of trying to outshine your boss when you give a presentation to his boss. Always give your boss credit in front of his boss, even if the credit was simply mentorship, guidance, or moral support.

2. His performance. Your boss doesn't want to make mistakes. He wants his performance to be at the highest level. He wants to meet his goals, and he wants to contribute to the overall success of the organization.

Your role: Help your boss by jumping in to complete projects if you can see they might be getting off-track. Help your colleagues if they are struggling with a specific task. Tell your boss when you think he's about to make a mistake.

3. His compliance. No matter what the level, your boss must be in compliance with employer policies, process timelines, state laws, and any other applicable requirements in his chosen profession. Failure to meet compliance requirements might remain hidden for a while, but could be the downfall of your boss if failures are public or severe. Compliance will be a concern especially if you work for a large organization. Large organizations tend to have more rules, regulations, and processes to follow.

Your role: Be acutely aware of compliance issues and keep your boss on track. Not all people are detail-oriented. If your boss isn't, then you must be a keeper of details. In addition, your boss is likely to find almost all compliance-related tasks to be boring. If your boss openly disdains "stupid" requirements, you can be the person who takes care of them so he doesn't have to. Offer to do the things your boss dislikes. Draft memos, performance assessments, revenue reports, and anything else your boss is likely to find mundane. Doing so will allow your boss to focus on the strategic initiatives that will help his career, which will help yours as well.

4. Skip-level issues. Skip-level refers to issues that are two organizational steps above your boss. For example, let's say that your boss has decided on a specific course of action. His boss was fine with it. But then one level above, complaints occur. Maybe someone powerful didn't like the decision. Your boss must always be thinking about how the higher-ups view his decisions as well. This is even more true if your boss's direct supervisor is not well-respected by the organization.

Your role: Help your boss by always considering the impact of his decisions on others in the organization. Make suggestions to improve a project or process. Find out everything you can about the powerful players in your organization so that you can always consider how they might view a decision.

5. Perceptions of others. Your boss must attend to the perceptions of people other than his boss. This is commonly known as a career "brand". When your boss's brand is positive, it will benefit him in a variety of ways. These benefits may include the ability to push projects through more easily, collaborate with other departments, and take risks on innovative ideas. Helping your boss cultivate a good brand will, by association, help your own career.

Your role: Speak positively about your boss to others. Compliment your boss during informal conversations with your colleagues. If you hear people criticize your boss, correct the perception if it's inaccurate. If it's true, then stay silent. If you must say anything, comment on how self-reflective your boss is and how he has improved that area over time.

6. Timeliness and project completion. Just like anyone else, your boss has projects he must complete and deadlines he must adhere to. High-profile projects must be done on time and must meet quality standards. In large organizations, most projects are intertwined with other departments. Thus, others may be relying upon your boss to complete his tasks before they can complete theirs.

Your role: You can help your boss by ensuring project and task completion. Offer to pitch in if you see one of his projects getting off-track. If you notice that a colleague's project is in danger, offer to help that person as well. Be involved with as many of your boss's projects as possible. This will give you the opportunity to notice any areas that could use help and to assist when necessary.

7. His promotional opportunities. Until you reach the highest positions in your organization, most bosses you have will wish to receive promotions themselves. If your boss likes you, this will be helpful to your career. You could be promoted to replace your boss, or your boss could hire you in his new job.

Your role. Be attentive to this need of your boss, unless he has assured you he has no desire to promote. When your boss is seeking a promotion, he may be more cautious or more focused on political decisions. Be supportive rather than critical of decisions that seem more political than practical. If you are helping your boss in all the other areas I've mentioned in this section, you will be helping your boss's opportunity to promote.

8. His priorities. Your boss may have priorities that puzzle you. You may think it's a big deal that two of your colleagues are fighting, because it will impact an upcoming deliverable. Your boss may think it's a silly disagreement between two immature employees. Conversely, what seems like an unimportant task to you may be a big deal to your boss. Your boss's priorities will usually be based upon potential business outcomes. But they also could be based on politics or issues that don't seem important to you.

Your role: Never assume you know your boss's priorities. Never minimize—or over-emphasize—a situation until you understand how your boss views it. Understand your boss's viewpoint by asking direct questions. This is easy to do by simply asking your boss, "Is this a priority for you?" If the answer you get makes it clear that it is not, follow up by asking, "Would you like me to take care of it for you?" If the answer makes it clear that the issue is a priority for your boss, follow up with, "Is there any way I can help you?" Your energy should be focused on helping your boss with his priorities as well as handling the lesser priorities your boss simply needs you to cross off the "to-do" list.

9. His relationships with other departments or divisions. It is likely that your boss must rely upon multiple departments to ensure his own success. Most high-profile projects require the effort of different leaders in the organization. If your boss's relationships with those leaders is contentious, his opportunity to execute on important initiatives will be negatively impacted. No one will want to collaborate with him. Worse yet, other leaders could even try to sabotage his work.

Your role: If your boss is a great relationship-builder, emulate and learn from the strategies he uses. Leverage his positive relationships and seek opportunities to work collaboratively with other departments. In this way, you will further expand his network. If your boss is more of an introvert, or if your boss has the type of personality that engenders conflict amongst other departments, you should be the relationship-builder. While remaining loyal to your boss, you can work behind the scenes to listen to others' opinions, take input, and build bridges. People will assume you are doing so on behalf of your boss, and your actions will help his endeavors.

10. Your relationships with other departments or divisions. Everything you do reflects upon your boss. If you create conflicts or problems with other leaders, you inhibit your boss's ability to bring his own initiatives to fruition. This is true even if your boss himself is less than skilled at being collaborative. Your boss doesn't want to deal with you being disliked or disrespected. If others complain about your work or your demeanor, it only creates additional work for your boss—work that he is likely to find distasteful or a waste of time.

Your role: Your boss might be incredibly loyal to you. You might be the hardest worker among all your peers. You might be the smartest, most strategic thinker. But if your own political mistakes begin to impact your boss, he will eventually need to distance himself from you. Cultivate and maintain relationships with multiple departments so that you can help your boss work collaboratively whenever necessary.

The last chapter explained how to think like your boss. Use the strategies to ensure your boss is promoting your career brand so that you'll be given opportunities to advance. The next chapter explains how you can also leverage other leaders in your organization to help your career.

Strategy #6: Be Strategic About Mentoring

Many new professionals wonder about how to get a mentor. And many busy executives are flooded with requests to be a mentor. This results in frustration on all parts. Less experienced professionals have difficulties finding someone to give them ongoing advice. More experienced professionals are reluctant to mentor due to the perceived time commitment of maintaining a mentoring "relationship".

In my view, the concept of having, and being, a "mentor" has become far too complicated. A mentorship need not be a formalized arrangement for a lengthy time period. A mentoring relationship can be informal, intermittent, and even spread out among several executives with different skills. You don't need to learn everything from one mentor. You can learn many different concepts from many different mentors throughout your entire career.

Ask yourself why you really want a mentor. You want a mentor to give you advice about your career. But there are so many different aspects to being successful that you'll probably be better off seeking a wider range of advice. One executive might be perfect for teaching you how to engage employees. Another might be more appropriate to help you improve your executive presence. If you only seek help from one person, you are limited to that one person's experience and opinions.

How to Ask for a Mentor

The key to finding effective mentors is to keep your options open. Expect to receive shorter chunks of information from a wider variety of people. Don't expect people to agree to a lengthy time commitment. Rather, simply ask an individual for advice on a specific topic.

See how the first meeting goes. If it goes well, you can ask for another meeting. If the executive isn't as helpful as you had hoped, you can just walk away after hearing his opinion on a few specific topics. If the executive seems very helpful, you can ask him to meet again on a different topic.

These steps will help you identify and meet with anyone who might have advice to help your career. Use these suggestions to get mentoring advice without a standard mentoring arrangement.

1. Choose five potential mentors who have some hiring influence. Be strategic, because the connection you make could lead to a job opportunity. The potential mentors could be in your organization, or they could work for a similar employer who might be hiring at some point. The mentor could be someone who might have a job opening in the future. The mentor could be someone who helps with hiring for other positions. It could be the person in charge of your department or division.

2. For each of the five, think what that individual might give you advice about. Try to keep the topic as specific as possible. But keep your questions about the topic as

broad as possible. For example, the topic might be about increasing sales. Your questions would be "What strategies have you used to increase sales? What have you learned about sales in your career? What do you think most people miss when they are trying to sell something? Do you have any advice for me about how I can improve my sales?"

3. In separate communications, request a meeting with each individual. In the email or phone call, state who you are, give a compliment related to the topic you're going to ask about, and then request a meeting on the topic. For example, your email might say, "Mr. Bossman, I am a sales associate in the contract sales division. My colleagues have shared that you have several years of experience in sales and are an expert regarding successful strategies. I would love to ask you some questions and learn from your experience. Would you be willing to meet with me for about an hour? I would come to your office at whatever day or time is convenient. If you don't have time to meet with me, is there another person you would recommend? Thank you so much for your time!"

4. If you know the person is really busy and unlikely to agree to a meeting with someone they don't know, try a different route. You might need to have your boss or another colleague who knows you both make the first introduction. Then you will take it from there.

5. If the meeting goes well, ask for a follow-up meeting. You can say, "Thank you so much for your time, you've been really helpful. If I have more questions after I try some of your strategies, could I meet with you again for follow-up?" If the meeting was just ho-hum, you can simply thank the person for their time, and then leave.

6. If you want a more extensive mentoring relationship at that point, you can ask for it. Only do so if you know

you've made a good impression and if you think you've connected with the individual. Be very specific about the time commitment and the duration of the mentoring relationship you're requesting. You could say, "You've been so helpful! Would you be willing to meet with me about once a month over the next six months or so? I'd love to get your thoughts on some other aspects of my career." Notice that you haven't actually used the words "would you be my mentor" but that's what you've asked for. And you've let the person know exactly how much of a time commitment you'd like.

In short, you don't need to have a formal mentoring relationship to get advice. In fact, many times it's better to get career wisdom from a variety of people. You'll expand your network of connections while gathering opinions from a wider variety of executives.

How to Be a Good Mentee

Because of my career in human resources and because of my books, I'm frequently asked to be a mentor. In some cases, it's for a short duration and a specific purpose, such as a job loss, a job search, or an interview. In other cases, I'm asked for an ongoing mentoring relationship.

I've noticed that not all mentees understand their role in a mentoring relationship. Some simply arrive at my office, sit down, and expect me to start, and maintain, the conversation. Some just look at me without taking notes, making me wonder if they are listening. Some neglect to read an article or do the short reflection I asked them to do before our next meeting.

Exhibit the behaviors below to ensure your mentor knows that you value the relationship and appreciate the time commitment.

1. Be prepared with questions. Don't expect your mentor to lead the conversation. You're the one who wants the help, so come prepared with questions. You can start with easy questions like asking your mentor about his professional background. Then you can move to more specific questions related to business strategies and advice.

2. Take notes. Taking notes shows you are listening. It also shows that the person's advice is important enough for you to write down. Don't have your head down writing all of the time, because you need to maintain eye contact, too. But do be sure to write down the main points being shared with you.

3. Follow up with meetings when asked. I almost always request that my mentees work with my assistant to schedule their own meetings. I expect that if the time is important to them, they will take the initiative to schedule the meetings they wanted. Recently one of my mentees asked to continue a formal coaching engagement beyond the scheduled time period. When I agreed, she immediately searched my calendar and sent invites for the next six months. I was impressed with her initiative! That is a great way to show your enthusiasm for the mentoring relationship.

3. Show interest in learning. You mentor might make suggestions for you to read a book, or engage in an activity. Whenever your mentor suggests something, show initiative to do it, even if you're not sure you want to. I'll never quiz anyone regarding whether or not they read a book I recommended. But I'm always impressed by people who come prepared to discuss what they learned from it. The same is true for activities. If your mentor suggests you write down all of your recent accomplishments over the past six months, then do so. Come prepared with the list at your next meeting. Your mentor will appreciate you took the time.

4. Don't skip meetings. It's completely fine if something comes up and you need to miss a session. But don't skip it without notifying your mentor in advance that you'll need to reschedule. Sometimes your mentor will need to miss a session as well. You should always be the one to follow up by rescheduling the missed meeting, regardless of who cancelled it.

5. Recognize time limits. The higher up your mentor is in the organization, the shorter your mentoring sessions are likely to be. For a mid-level vice president, it's probably OK to request an hour. For c-suite executives, be more realistic and request a half-hour only. If they want to schedule an hour, they will. When you're in the session, keep track of time. Don't begin a new discussion topic if your session is scheduled to be over in the next few minutes.

6. Be smart about your mentor's role in your organization. Always remember that this is a professional relationship, not a personal friendship. Although you'll probably develop trust with your mentor, now is not the time to share your personal faults. Nor should you over-emphasize your professional shortcomings. Your mentor is a person who has the potential to advocate for you in the organization. Don't give any information that will take away from his ability to do so. Learning from your mentor doesn't require you to share your weaknesses. Also, keep in mind that, unfortunately, not all mentors are as trustworthy as you would expect. If you are having serious professional challenges, pay for an outside executive coach. If your personal life is in shambles, pay for a therapist.

7. Be open to different mentors having different skillsets. Some mentors have been trained in executive coaching. Their approach is likely to be different from those without that level of specialization. Some mentors might just

focus on giving advice. Some might be more tactical, and some might be more strategic. Some might even be a little therapeutic, helping you to understand why you approach situations in a specific way. Go into the relationship with an open mind. Even if your mentor's approach isn't your favorite, you can align your questions to match his skills. Remember that having a mentor is always an opportunity to learn.

8. Keep the duration of your mentoring relationship relatively short. I recommend that when you ask your mentor for regular meetings, you give a specific end date. I further recommend that the overall duration be six months or less. Even three sessions over three months is a reasonable request. You can always request to extend the time if you believe your mentor's ongoing advice would be especially helpful. I recently had someone schedule a call with me for a quick advice session on one topic. After that session, she requested another in two months, saying, "After that, I might want your input again in another few months." I loved how she approached it. First, she only requested the time needed to get the specific advice she wanted from me. Second, she let me know exactly how many other sessions would help her. Of course I agreed.

9. Consider call-in mentoring. If you have a company that's spread out geographically, having regular phone calls is an easy, and convenient, option for you and your mentor. You could call-in every other session, or as a regular communication method. My longest mentoring relationship was with a new human resources executive located six hours away, on the other side of my state. She had been an executive in another role, but hadn't run a human resources department before. She requested that for the first six months of her new job, we speak every Friday

morning for a half-hour. She wanted to run decisions by me and get my thoughts on how to handle different situations. I agreed. The six months, by mutual agreement, turned into five years of regular, call-in mentoring. Then, when she moved to my city, the five years turned into a professional friendship that has now lasted over ten years. At this point, the advice goes both ways, and we enjoy helping each other think through difficult situations.

10. Show appreciation. Your mentor doesn't need lavish gifts or even coffee cards. But, at a minimum, show your appreciation by saying thank you at the end of each session. You can also write a note to share how valuable your mentor's advice has been to you. But one of the best ways to show appreciation to your mentor is to tell his boss, your boss, and other leaders, about your positive mentoring experience. When I discover that one of my mentees has complimented me to someone else, it's the best thank you I can receive!

How to Have a Safe Mentoring Relationship

The ethical leaders I've known aren't committing sexual harassment. Nevertheless, their desire to mentor has been hindered by prominent sexual harassment news stories. They worry about false accusations, and they worry about the perceptions of others. This is unfortunate, and it hurts those who would otherwise benefit from a mentoring relationship.

There are strategies you can take to ensure that your own mentoring relationship is safe from accusations, or perceptions, of sexual harassment. First, understand that on the continuum of sexual harassment, the most common allegations are not of the "quid pro quo" kind.

The most common accusations occur within the context of what I call sexual privilege. I define sexual privilege as using positional power to garner sexual attention, or using sexual power to garner career attention.

In my experience, sexual privilege perceptions are a more common problem than sexual harassment allegations. And they negatively impact both men and women, of any sexual orientation. Executives worry that their mentorship of an attractive (usually younger) subordinate will be perceived as the executive seeking a sexual relationship. Subordinates worry that coworkers will assume their promotion came via a mentorship that turned sexual. Executives don't want to be seen as using power-based sexual privilege. Subordinates don't want to be seen as using attractiveness-based sexual privilege.

I've had many male mentors in my career who never exhibited one hint of sexual privilege. That didn't stop others from accusing them—and me—of using it. One particular nasty comment, said as a "joke" at a bar, was that I had gotten my promotion "on my knees" with my male mentor. It didn't matter that the specific mentor had nothing to do with hiring for the position I received.

I cried over that one. Much later in my career, I realized just how often those "jokes" are made. And I finally quit crying over it.

Almost every female executive I know has, at some point in her career, been accused of using attractiveness to get a promotion or develop a mentorship with a powerful male executive. And almost every male executive I know has, at some point in his career, been accused of using positional power to develop a relationship with an attractive subordinate under the guise of mentorship.

Male or female, the more it happens to you, the more you avoid doing anything that might give the appearance of sexual privilege. Sometimes, you end up avoiding mentoring relationships entirely.

Don't do that. It will limit your networking and learning opportunities. Instead, follow my safe mentoring guidelines. These practical actions will reduce the chances of sexual privilege accusations occurring.

1. Make sure your mentors comprise a diverse group. If you request advice from three women, ask for advice from three men also. You will enhance the perception of sexual privilege if you request mentoring from only one gender.

2. Consider asking for a mentor's advice in small groups you have organized. When requesting generalized career advice, promotion tips, and company culture, there is no reason you cannot gather that wisdom in groups of two or three. This will allow you to be seen as a leader of others, one with a collaborative nature.

3. When being mentored one-on-one by someone others might perceive as being attracted to you, request to meet in public places. Offer to have coffee or lunch. Those who want to leverage sexual privilege seek to hide meetings. Holding mentoring sessions in public places where others can see you helps prevent the perception of secrecy.

4. Stick to daylight meetings. It might be more comfortable or more convenient to meet for drinks after work, but these meetings are huge gossip magnets. Even if you are meeting in a small group, the presence of alcohol and the absence of daylight can create a negative perception of your intentions.

5. Never drive in the same car unless in a small group. If you and your mentor are leaving from the same office, it might seem odd to take separate cars. If that's

the case, then make up an excuse of an errand you have to run after lunch.

6. Use only work or office cell phones, and avoid texting as much as possible. Exchanging private contact information with a mentor could give the impression you want a more personal relationship. Texting is a more informal form of communication that can also imply a closer relationship. On the other hand, work cell phones are easily tracked. When you only use work cell phone numbers, you make it clear there is nothing you would text that you wouldn't mind anyone reading.

7. Keep the focus on work and career-related topics only. As you get to know your mentor better, the two of you might feel more comfortable joking with each other or sharing personal anecdotes. That's understandable, but be sure the conversation is 90% related to the mentorship. This keeps both people focused on the reason for the relationship and helps prevent the possibility that either will leverage sexual privilege.

8. Be especially cautious in work-related social situations. Include your spouse or partner as much as possible. Develop a reputation for complete commitment, speak positively of your spouse/partner, and introduce your mentor to him/her whenever possible. If you are single, develop a persona of staying sober and leaving earlier than most. The appearance of sexual privilege is enhanced by executives and mentees (attached or single) drinking excessively and being the last to leave social functions. You'd rather be accused of being boring than be accused of leveraging your attractiveness for personal gain.

9. If you think your mentor is developing a crush on you, or if your mentor has hinted at a more personal connection, stop the relationship. Don't make a big deal

about it. The best strategy is to email, "I feel like we've had good conversations, and I have gotten such great advice from you. But I know how busy you are, and I don't want to take up more of your valuable time. Thank you so much for your help over the past few months!"

The reason it should be in email is twofold. First, there is finality in email; there is no room for argument. Most importantly, email creates a record that you are the one who ended the mentoring relationship. You need to do this in order to protect yourself should your former mentor retaliate against you in some way. It's highly unlikely it will happen, but remember, this is one way illegal sexual harassment occurs. Hopefully, your mentor will be smart and walk away from the relationship gracefully.

10. As an overall strategy, imagine a person who wants to use his/her attractiveness to exercise sexual privilege. Then, do the exact opposite. You don't keep the relationship a secret. You don't meet alone in secluded places. You welcome others to your meetings. You don't socialize after hours.

This chapter has taught you the importance of being mentored. You have also gained skills to be a good mentee and to ensure a safe mentoring relationship. The next chapters will focus on expanded networking skills. You will learn the importance of networking with other colleagues in your profession, and how to develop and maintain those connections.

Strategy #7: Connect Up, Across, and Down

Up to this point, you've learned work strategies that will get you promoted. You are in control of those activities. But you don't work in a silo. It will be difficult for you to get promoted if the right people don't see or know about the good work you're doing. In addition, if you suffer a setback in your career, you will need to leverage others' expertise, access, and knowledge to get yourself back on track.

For those important reasons, the next three chapters focus on your interactions with others. Chapter 7 explains what a networking web is, and who should be in your sphere of influence. Chapter 8 focuses on strategies to help you connect. If you're an introvert, or if you feel uncomfortable meeting new people, you'll find plenty of useful suggestions to help you on a daily basis. In Chapter 9, I explain the ways you can maintain your professional connections across companies, industries, and geographical regions.

The Networking Web

There is a reason why the verb for getting to know others who may be in a position to help you is called networking. When doing this activity, you are, in fact, working a net or a web of contacts. It's much like that old shampoo commercial--someone who can help your career might tell one friend, who tells one friend, who tells another friend, and so on.

Helping your career could mean referring you for a promotional opportunity. Helping your career could mean referring you for a new job if you get laid off. Helping your career could mean saying good things about your work to people who might have a future opening.

Think broadly about the purposes of your networking web. It's not just about getting you a promotion. It's about having a broad base of supporters who can assist you whenever you need it, for whatever you need. You can lean on the one who can help you the most at that time period.

Note that I don't call networking a funnel, nor a ladder. If you only network up your line of authority, you will be seen as a climber. People will think you only connect to others because of the power they hold. If you only network with those who work for you, people may think you lack the confidence to work or socialize with power players. And, if you only network vertically--up the career ladder or down the career ladder--you will neglect valuable contacts with peers in other companies or industries.

You also need to ensure diversity among the people you network with. If others see you as only belonging to one group, it's less likely they will hire you to work with people outside of that group. Diversify your networking web by making connections across races, genders, sexual orientations, age, and political affiliations.

Imagine you're a 28-year-old white male. Naturally, your closest friends at work are a group of other 20-somethings. There a few women in your group, but you are all white. Now imagine there is a promotion opportunity in a different department. There, you would be working with, and in some cases supervising, a mostly older, male crowd. They are very racially diverse.

Even if you've interviewed well, it's likely the interview panel will be asking themselves, "How do we know he can get along in our department? He doesn't seem to have much interest in working with the older generation, and it doesn't look like he has any experience working with a racially diverse group." This is one of the many reasons you must proactively reach out to diverse groups.

Always remember that in a web, you can work up, down, across, and even through the middle. In a web, if one string breaks, you can step across and find a different path. In a web, you are supported by the strength of multiple ties, none of which is your sole support.

You may be discouraged thinking about your own networking web. You might be thinking you don't know anyone other than the people in your department. Perhaps you're an introvert and don't socialize much. All of that might be true. Just start where you are, and get moving!

You probably have more contacts in your networking web than you think. There are many more people you know besides those on your cell phone. Friends and family are a sure bet to help you in any circumstance. Start with them first. Where do they work? Who do they know? Who do they go to church with?

When appropriate, tell them about your work, what your projects are, and your successes. Be sure they hear in your voice how much you love your job. Don't tell them anything negative—when you need to leverage your contacts, you want them to view you as a successful professional.

You also need to identify individuals in your own organization. Think of those who know you well enough to mention your name to a hiring manager. These are individuals you've worked with on one or more projects. Knowing you well enough means a person who can provide at least one positive trait about you.

In my roles, I have frequently been asked for names of people who are ready for "the next step". I am also asked by candidates to refer their names to other hiring managers. I am always happy to do both. Why? Because I know many people well enough to give their name to a hiring manager. All someone has to do is ask. And that's very common.

Human resources personnel in your organization are typically asked to provide input, even if they aren't directly hiring. Get to know them. Impress them with your work, and that connection will always benefit you.

If I know the candidate well, I will provide my assessment as a reference. It's ideal if I have worked with the person on a project or issue. Then I can comment on their work. If I don't know the candidate well, I am still happy provide my impression of any limited interactions. For example, I might say, "I met Carla when we hired her as Jim's receptionist. Although I don't work with her directly and can't tell you about her professional skills, she always seems very friendly and helpful. I'm not sure exactly what type of candidate you want, but her resume is worth taking a look at."

In order to formalize your networking opportunities, I recommend that you actually draw a web of connections. Start with you in the center of the web. Now draw lines for all of your work connections—bosses, coworkers, other colleagues. Be sure to include people from your former work roles and any professional groups you belong to. Then add lines for friends. Include their connections to professionals in your area. Do the same with your family.

Include their coworkers, bosses, and colleagues.

Be very broad in your thinking about what your network is going to do for you. It will help you advance, for sure. But it can help you in times of trouble as well.

Let's say you're not particularly happy with your current boss. You're looking, but you haven't applied. It's not unrealistic for your aunt to ask a question on your behalf. (This is assuming your aunt loves you, and you got her a birthday card last year).

She might say to her boss, "Hey my nephew Tom is looking for a new opportunity. He's a great guy with skills in sales and marketing. Do you have any colleagues who are hiring in that area?"

You can also ask professional acquaintances for a referral. If there is a position available where they work, you might say, "I know we haven't worked together, but I would like to ask you for a small favor. I would appreciate it if you could refer me to your hiring manager. I'm hoping if you do so, he might take a look at my application and resume. I know they get so many it's probably hard for them to screen through them all!"

If you feel uncomfortable asking for a referral, think about how you would feel if you were asked. Usually, you are happy to help out someone--after all, you're only giving a name. It's just a small favor. People will feel the same when you ask them.

Other than your own hard work, your networking web will be the single greatest tool to help advance your career so you can retire early. To reiterate, it's not enough just to do a great job. Other people have to know you're doing a great job. That's what networking is all about.

Don't make the mistake of assuming you can slack on networking just because one person in the organization likes you. If you never network, no one else is going to feel connected to you, and that will make it difficult for you to get a promotion.

On the other hand, don't rely on networking alone to help your career. Without great work to back it up, you'll be seen as an insincere suck-up. Always ensure that your professional skills and work ethic are apparent to others. In short, do a great job, and make sure others know you're doing it.

Connect with Influencers

You should be networking at all stages of your career. But when you know it's time to promote or advance, you need to embark upon very deliberate networking with influencers. Influencers are those who may be asked to weigh in on a hiring decision.

Some people aren't sure how to approach powerful individuals. It's true that usually those in influential positions are very busy. Many times they are difficult to access because there are layers of people who work for them. Each layer has someone whose job it is to give the influential person more time for strategic endeavors. The more influential the person, the more layers you need to go through.

In this circumstance, unless you work for a very small organization, plan your networking strategy with influencers in advance. Prioritize influential individuals to contact as follows:

1. Within your departmental area, identify the company leader in charge of the department, if that person interacts directly with your level of position by running meetings, setting strategy, or organizing departmental work. If you

are at a level that does not interact with that person, choose the highest-level person in your department who guides your everyday work the most.

2. Also within your departmental area, identify influential people who are at your same level, who may be in a different business unit, and who you believe are likely to be promoted in the near future. If those people are indeed promoted, it will increase your connections to influencers in other business units.

3. Going outside your departmental area, identify influential people who are no more than one supervisory level above your position.

4. Going outside your departmental area, identify influential people at your level who may have general insight into the company and who you believe are likely to be promoted in the near future.

Once you have identified these individuals, use multiple strategies to make the connection. These strategies will help them get to know you better. It can look odd if, out of the blue, you invite someone you don't even know to lunch. Thus, it is ideal if you have an authentic opportunity to meet the person such as in a meeting or at a professional event.

Offer to work on additional projects or serve on committees. Offer to help be a volunteer, note-taker, or logistical expert. Offer to investigate or research a specific idea or initiative in order to provide background or context. In short, make yourself available to do work that others don't have the time nor the desire to do.

In this way, you will encounter influential leaders naturally. You don't have to force the initial encounter. When later you do request a one-on-one, ensure that there is a purpose for the meeting. Make sure it is a request the individual will find compelling and interesting.

In addition, I recommend only asking for a half-hour of their time. If the person is very busy, a half-hour won't seem too intrusive, but it will give you an opportunity to learn and make a connection. The following are potential reasons to ask for a meeting:

1. To gather the person's perspective on a specific initiative you are working on.

2. To gather the person's advice regarding potential career pathways within the company.

3. To gain the person's insight about your line of business or line of work.

4. To ask the person for advice regarding a decision you need to make, for example, deciding to take a promotion in one area or the other.

Finally, don't forget to network with those who hold positions that are at a lower level than yours. Some of the high fliers in that group could be in a position to refer you to your desired job at some point in the future.

Those in positions lower than yours might not be the ones actually doing the hiring. But they will certainly put in a good word for you if they viewed you as a trusted colleague or mentor. An added bonus is that it feels good to "pay it forward" to others and be the person they look to for a referral!

Strategy #8: Use Multiple Connection Strategies

In this chapter, I provide you with a variety of ways to connect with others. If you are naturally quiet, you can use these strategies to initiate a conversation. If you are naturally outgoing, use these strategies to be sure you're focused on learning about others rather than only talking about yourself.

When your colleagues believe you like them beyond their work contributions, it creates a connection that will survive any minor work-related frustrations. Your relationship will lay the groundwork to collaborate or to work through problems. Your relationships will also lay the groundwork for connections to those in hiring positions. This will put you in a good position should a promotion become available.

Not all colleagues will want to share details about their personal lives. However, all will appreciate you showing genuine interest and positive regard. Think about it—when you know your supervisor and your colleagues genuinely like you, it makes work more fun.

You can use a variety of ways to connect. Not all connection has to be verbal. You can create a positive environment just by your overall demeanor on good days, bad days, successful days, and days of failure.

Use your networking web to make a list of people you should be connecting with. It's easy to "forget" certain coworkers because they are quiet, or maybe you haven't gotten along with them in the past. Keeping a list helps you be accountable to yourself for making connections with a diverse group.

Once you've made your list of people you need to connect with, use the strategies in this chapter to tailor your interactions to their specific situation, preferences and interests.

Verbal Connection Strategies

1. Ask for their opinion and listen for the answer: work related.
- What do you think?
- What would you do?
- How would you approach this?
- What would best work for you?
- What do you think could be better?
- How do you feel about this?
- What do you think the impact would be if we?
- Tell me more about that.

2. Ask for an update and listen for answers and details: non-work related.
- How was your weekend?
- What did you do?
- How are your kids?
- How is your husband/wife/partner/boyfriend/girlfriend?
- Did you have a fun time at _____ event?

- Have you seen any good movies lately?
- How are your dogs/cats/pets?
- Did you need any help with _____?
- How is your mom/dad/sister/brother/grandma/grandpa doing?

3. Ask about their career goals.
    - Where do you see you next job being?
    - Have you considered applying for a promotion?
    - What other areas interest you?
    - I think you would be great for promotional opportunities, how can I help?
    - What is holding you back from seeking a promotion? How can I help?
    - I think you would be great for _____ opportunity. Are you interested?

4. Ask about personal goals.
    - How is the health focus going? Can I help?
    - How is the house search going?
    - What goals did you set for yourself this year?
    - Do you have anything you're working on this year?

5. Revisit key details in follow-up conversations to show you were listening.
    - How was your visit with your mom? How is she doing?
    - Is your son/daughter enjoying middle school?
    - How is your son's soccer (sports) team doing?
    - Did your daughter get into that Advanced Placement/Honors class she wanted to?
    - How are the kids doing with the move to the new school?
    - Did you end up going to Newport Beach for spring break? How was it?
    - I brought you a healthy snack because you said you were trying to eat better.

- I know you like the LA Lakers, and I saw this bumper sticker and got it for you.

6. Offer sincere compliments.
   - Coworkers don't always need to be complimented on their work. Find other reasons to give a verbal compliment.
   - Consider complimenting a coworker on achieving a personal goal he/she set.
   - Consider complimenting an employee on his/her children, commitment to community service, or time spent caring for his/her sick parent.

7. Find common ground.
   - Find similarities between you and your coworker.
   - Find similar likes or preferences in terms of anything from sports teams to food favorites.
   - Find similar personal characteristics such as children, pets, or family members.

Non-Verbal Connection Strategies

Below are some non-verbal strategies you can use to connect with people in your network. These actions support the conversation and add sincerity to each interaction.

1. Smile at your coworkers. It's easy to get caught up in your own thoughts when you walk by your coworkers. But when you don't smile, coworkers might automatically assume they are the cause of your lackluster attitude—or your displeasure.

2. Make eye contact. When you are talking, really look at the person you're speaking with. Notice his/her smile or lack thereof. If your colleague seems a little down, ask about it. You might say, "Are you feeling OK?" or "You seem a little down today, is everything alright?"

3. Offer your hand for a handshake. When you offer your hand for a handshake, you make an immediate connection. Your colleague will see you as approachable and wanting to connect with him/her.

4. Meet your coworker on his/her "turf". Many times, especially if we are the boss, we have meetings in our own offices or areas. This automatically sets up an unspoken power differential. To help that, go to the other person's office or area to say hi or to meet him/her. Make an effort to walk around "just to see how everyone is doing."

5. Keep your arms and stance open when speaking with employees. When you cross your arms in front of you, look down and/or otherwise "close" your body language, you will seem "closed" to members of your network. Instead, keep your arms open and to your side.

6. Nod and make eye contact when anyone is speaking to you. Even if you're short on time, be sure that when someone is speaking to you, it's clear that you are listening. If you do need to cut the conversation short, say, "I'm sorry, I have an appointment to get to. I want to follow up on this, however. When would be a good time to talk again?"

7. Put away your phone. When speaking with anyone else, do not answer or look at your phone unless an emergency. If you do need to look at your phone, explain why. You can say, "I'm really sorry I need to check this text, but I need to make sure my son has a ride home." After you do so, put your phone away again and turn your full focus back to your colleague.

8. Turn off or look away from your computer screen. If you are at a computer when someone comes to talk to you, stand up or move away from it so that the person knows you are giving him/her your full attention. If you can't walk

away from the computer, try to turn off the screen or tilt the screen away from the conversation.

9. Add emotion to your voice and tone. Be sure your tone of voice matches the message you are delivering. If you say "I'm so sorry you are feeling that way," be sure your tone sounds sorry. If you say, "That is so awesome! I'm glad your son won the game!" be sure your tone sounds happy.

10. Before having a conversation with a person you find difficult to connect with, imagine having the conversation with someone you care about, like your spouse or your child. How would you treat that person? What tone would you use? Then try to channel that feeling when interacting with the difficult person.

In the Moment Connection Strategies

When you notice and comment on specific events in someone's life (good and bad), it shows that you care. It shows that you noticed. Most importantly, it shows your work connections that you value them as unique individuals, not just people who can help your career.

Here are some events you can "notice" that will help you connect with members of your network. You can notice them by a sympathetic comment, a kind word, or another recognition, as applicable.

1. Birthdays, anniversaries.
2. Work anniversaries.
3. Illnesses: "I'm so sorry you were out sick. I hope you are feeling better!" This can be for your colleague's illness, children's illnesses or other close family members.
4. Failures and mistakes: "Yep, that didn't go so well. But it's so great that you tried. I'm sure it will be better the

next time." Say it with a smile on your face and a genuinely supportive tone in your voice.

6. Completion of a project.
7. Helping another coworker.
8. Contributing effort more than expected.
9. Close family member weddings.
10. Divorces.
11. New home, new apartment.
12. New car, new "big purchase".
13. Child adoptions, birthdays, graduations and weddings.
14. Pet adoptions, birthdays, deaths.
15. Family member funerals/death. Rudy Guliani says, "Weddings optional. Funerals mandatory."
16. A "bad day" for whatever reason.
17. A "great day" for whatever reason.

Strategy #9: Maintain Your Professional Relationships

Now you know how to develop a professional network to help you throughout your career. Maintaining those relationships is equally important. This will be relatively easy with those who work for your same employer. But you'll need to be more proactive to do the same for other colleagues.

You can't just sit back and ignore the professional relationships you've established. In this chapter I'll describe strategies to ensure that once you create a professional network, your contacts will be there when you need them most.

Maintain Professional Friendships

You will certainly derive personal satisfaction from your connections with others. Aside from that, there are also several very practical reasons to do so.

First, maintaining friendships with colleagues who work for other employers gives you information about possible promotion opportunities. Let's say you work for Marriott hotels, and your friend Larry works for Hilton hotels. Larry can tell you what jobs may come open before they get posted. He might even get you an informal interview with the manager before anyone else.

Larry will also be able to give you a general idea of the pay ranges, and which jobs at Hilton pay more than your job at Marriott. This is important in the private sector, because you don't want to waste your time applying for a job that you end up not taking because of the low pay.

Then, if you do get a job with Larry's employer Hilton, you have someone to help your transition. Larry can tell you about the culture there and the unstated "rules" people follow. He can introduce you to other people at Hilton so you don't feel alone.

Finally, your friendship with Larry ensures that if you lose your job at Marriott, you have a connection in another major hotel chain. Hopefully, you have more friends, like Larry, who will refer you to their own employers. This will allow you to get a new job more quickly, minimizing your time without a paycheck. Decreasing your money-saving "down" time will increase your ability to retire wealthy when you want to.

Throughout my career, I have known several people who were fired or laid off by their organizations. Those who had maintained positive relationships with other professionals in their industry weren't unemployed for long. Their relationships helped them prepare for job interviews, get referrals, and ultimately, get hired very quickly by someone else.

It's not just your peers or hiring authorities you should maintain contacts with, however. Be sure to maintain friendships with people who worked for you as well. If they move on to other employers, they will at least be able to give you a verbal reference as a great boss or innovative worker. This will increase your chances of getting an interview.

Maintaining professional friendships doesn't take a large time commitment. If you're an introvert, you may not be comfortable having people around you all the time. If you're a single parent, or someone with large family commitments, you might not have the time to cultivate multiple outside friendships. Don't worry! Just take the actions below to get maximum benefit with minimal effort.

1. Be sure to maintain the work friendships you have at your current employer. Be a nice, positive, collaborative and contributing member of the team. This way, if any of your colleagues leave to work for another employer, you know they will speak positively about you.

2. Keep a list of your closest colleagues who leave to work for another employer. Make it a habit to invite them for lunch or coffee once every six months, just to catch up.

3. Attend professional meetings that have employees from multiple employers present in order to keep connections with those individuals. Take time to have personal conversations before and after the meeting.

4. Schedule sending an email or text at least once a year to each professional friend you used to work with. You can wish them a happy holiday season, ask how they are doing, and tell them you hope their new job is going well.

5. Make phone calls to your former colleagues to ask for advice, get a different perspective, or ask for someone else's opinion. People love being asked to give their advice. This type of connection is authentic while giving you the opportunity to connect.

Maintain An Active Online Presence

Another way to maintain professional friendships, and to cultivate more awareness about your "brand" overall, is to maintain an active social media presence.

Even if you don't connect in-person with former colleagues, your online presence and posting will keep you on their mind. When a former colleague recently asked me for some interview help, I was more than willing to do so. Although I hadn't actually spoken to her in two years, we had been Facebook friends and LinkedIn connections. It felt like we had maintained a connection, even though we hadn't done so in person.

That said, be a smart social media magnet. Avoid making social media mistakes that damage your brand. Instead, leverage social media's power to help your brand and maintain professional contacts.

First, I'll list what to avoid. Then, I'll list what you can do to help your brand and to maintain professional connections using each popular social media platform.

As a general rule, don't post anything that could be controversial or polarizing. Don't post during your workday, and never rant on social media. "Reposting" or "retweeting" is the same as posting yourself. Content you should avoid posting includes the below, but this is by no means a comprehensive list. When in doubt, leave it out.

What not to post:

1. Sexual innuendos or jokes.
2. Postings that advocate or disparage one political party or another.
3. Pictures/videos where you are scantily clothed.
4. Pictures/videos where you look drunk or have alcohol in your hand.

5. Negative comments or innuendos about your employer, your boss or coworkers.

6. Negative comments or innuendos about your former employer, former boss, or former coworkers.

7. Negative comments or innuendos about your ex-spouse, his/her new spouse or new romantic partner, or negative or sarcastic comments about their life in general.

8. Comments or jokes about any race, gender, ethnicity, country, sexual orientation or other special group.

9. Negative or sarcastic comments regarding news stories, media figures, or political figures.

10. Comments that give the impression you are sad, depressed, angry or otherwise unhappy with your life, family members, or work.

11. Comments that express negativity toward any one person, any institution, or any group.

What you can post:

On the flip side, here are the things you can and in some cases should post about within the parameters of various social media venues.

Facebook, Instagram and Snapchat

1. Positive comments about your family, friends, and coworkers.

2. Fun events you attend at work or outside of work.

3. Inspiring quotes or positive videos.

4. Comments designed to inspire or help others.

5. Weddings, graduations, birthdays, anniversaries and other special occasions.

6. Funny jokes or stories that do not disparage anyone else.

7. Congratulations, thank-yous and kudos to others, including family, friends, coworkers and bosses.

8. Dogs, cats, and other cute furry animals.

9. Food and restaurants.

10. Travel, landscapes, and scenery.

Twitter:

1. Same content as above can be tweeted if it is your personal account, but place more emphasis on work-related topics. (Be sure to add to your twitter account: "Tweets are my own" to be clear you are not tweeting as a representative of your employer.)

2. News people might want to know.

3. Retweets of your employer's posts if on positive topics.

4. Tweets mentioning positive events your employer wants to promote: job fairs, hiring, advertising campaigns, charity work, social responsibility work.

5. Positive retweets when you, your family, your employer or your coworkers win an award, take a new job, or accomplish something else positive.

LinkedIn:

1. Articles you wrote, if well-written, on career-related topics. These are an especially effective way to keep people aware of your career brand.

2. Links to positive articles about your current or former employer, with your complimentary comments.

3. Links to useful or informative articles on career-related topics.

4. Short posts to give a career-related piece of information, make a comment or provide a non-controversial opinion.

5. Photos, but only those that focus on a positive work-related event or news item.

To summarize, you can leverage your social media presence to keep in touch with professional contacts inside and outside of your own company. You never know when you might need an extra referral or other help to get you a job. Thus, maintaining these contacts is critical if you want to ensure a steady income stream with no gaps.

Strategy #10: Be Your Own Retirement Planning Expert

By now you know that a critical part of retiring wealthy is ensuring that your career advances so that your salary increases. You also know to maintain your network. Your network will help accelerate your career advancement. And, should you lose your job, your professional connections can help keep your time without a salary to a minimum. This will keep your retirement savings moving upward.

The majority of this book has been focused on teaching you strategies to help you achieve success in these important goals. But all the money in the world isn't going to help you retire wealthy if you don't actively plan for your retirement. And that means starting early, staying the course, and being disciplined about retirement from your first day on the job.

You're reading this book, so I know you're already motivated to do well in your career. You must leverage that same self-discipline to plan for a wealthy retirement. I'm not a financial planner. But I have, from the age of 30, been planning for my retirement.

It's not that I don't like work; in fact I love my career. I simply like planning for the time when it becomes a choice to go to work every day. With retirement comes the freedom to do as I choose: work or not, write or not, travel or not. It also gives me peace of mind knowing that if I were to lose my job, or if my husband were to lose his, we would be fine because of how much we have saved.

If you're early in your career, you can plan for multiple retirement date scenarios. Some can be aggressively optimistic: retire by 50. Some can be conservatively pessimistic: retire by 70. You should plan for the earliest retirement option you can find a way to achieve. Once you achieve that goal, you have the freedom to work, or not.

When you set a retirement goal that works for you, you'll find yourself focusing more on all of your career decisions. You'll begin to see that the more proactive you are implementing the strategies in this book, the more money you'll make. And the more money you make, the more choices you'll have for retirement.

After reading this chapter, the multiple impacts of any major career decision will become obvious. You'll see the impact of not leaving if you have a boss who isn't supporting your desire for a promotion. You'll see the impact of being unemployed if you have no professional network and you lose your job. And you'll see the impact of developing and maintaining a professional brand that will open up your career advancement opportunities.

The strategies I've laid out in this book are not about getting promoted just to get more power. They are about getting promoted, to get more money, to save more money, to have more options for your retirement.

In this chapter, I'll give you some basics about retirement planning within the context of making career choices. In each section, I'll explain how your career and savings actions right now will impact your future retirement scenario.

I'll first show you how to determine the amount of money you'll need in your retirement. I'll then provide you with different savings and career choices you can make to achieve various retirement outcomes. Finally, I'll summarize the common do's and don'ts for retirement planning.

My advice on retirement planning is for you to begin thinking about what you want, and how much money you need to save, in the context of your career choices. I am not a professional financial planner. For professional advice regarding your specific financial situation, rates of return, and investment options, do your own research or consult with a certified investment or financial planning professional.

Choose Your Preferred Retirement Lifestyle

Deciding how much money you want in retirement is the first step to planning it. If you're relatively young, your number can be whatever you want depending on the specific retirement lifestyle you expect. If you're over 40, you'll need to choose a number that is do-able within your retirement timeframe.

Your choices in retirement are all dependent upon two factors. The main factor is how many years you have to save before you retire. The second factor is what you want your annual income to be during retirement. Keep this in mind when determining the second factor: the smaller the annual income you live on now, the easier it is to save for retirement. Both points are illustrated in this section.

The information below, from an article by Kathleen Elkins at CNBC, demonstrates how the age at which you start saving for retirement greatly impacts the amount you have to save monthly. In her example, this is how much you would have to save each month to have $1 million by age 40, starting at age 20. You can see how the age you start saving makes a big difference.

At a six percent annual return, here's how much you would have to save:
$2,153 a month, if you start at age 20
$3,421 a month, if you start at age 25
$6,071 a month, if you start at age 30
$14,261 a month, if you start at age 35

You can see that the amount you have to save differs greatly with even a relatively small five-year delay. In her example, you have to save over $8,000 *less* per month if you start saving at 30 versus starting at 35!

You probably won't be saving $6,000 per month at age 30, no matter what you do. But you can see that the earlier you start saving, the less you have to save per month. This is because compounding interest, reinvested into future savings, adds up quickly over time.

Another concept to keep in mind is that whatever you save, you will learn to live on the lesser amount. So the amount of income you require to live on is the amount leftover after you've put aside money for retirement.

Here's an example to illustrate that point. Let's say you make $100,000 per year. If you're saving $20,000 of that for retirement each year, then really, you're living on $80,000 per year. So you only have to earn $80,000 per year in retirement, not $100,000.

How will you earn that $80,000 in retirement? There is an easy way for you to figure that out. The most common, and easiest, retirement planning strategy is to assume that you'll need $1 million in retirement savings for each $40,000 in income you want in retirement. This allows you to keep the original million (called the "principal") while living off of 4% interest per year.

So for this scenario, if you want to live on $80,000 in retirement, you'll need to have $2 million saved by the time you retire. In other words, $2 million will generate you $80,000 ($40,000 per million) in income each year—without touching the principal.

Now let's return to that really important factor: the amount of time you have to save before your retirement. How long will it take you to save $2 million? If you start at age 45 and want to retire at age 65, you would have to save $4,000 per month ($48,000 per year) from age 45 to 65. That would probably be really tough to do. But if instead you started saving at age 40, just five years earlier, you would only need to save $2600 per month ($31,200 per year) to hit your target of $2 million.

Are you reading this book at the very start of your career? If so, look at how little you need to save if you want to retire at age 60 on a reasonable $120,000 per year (in today's dollars). To get that, you're shooting for around $3 million. In this scenario, I assume a 6.25% rate of return, which is somewhat conservative. The stock market has actually averaged 10% returns over its lifetime. Most financial professionals recommend assuming a 6-7% return on investment when planning for retirement.

Start at age 25: $2,000
Start at age 30: $2,850
Start at age 35: $4,200
Start at age 40: $6,350
Start at age 45: $10,200
Start at age 50: $18,300

Now you know about the importance of starting to save early in your career so that you can retire when you want. Unfortunately, many people are unable to start saving early. For some, it's because they don't understand the importance of budgeting. For others, they simply don't make enough money to begin saving at a young age. And some people have suffered life circumstances that ruin their savings or prevent them from saving at all.

The next section shows you options for retirement based on the career choices you've made or could make. What you do now in your career, whether you're 25 years old or 45 years old, will impact your retirement options. If you follow my career advice in this book, you'll make more money, so you'll have more options. If you've made some mistakes along the way, or if you've had some bad luck, you'll have fewer options.

The key for you is to know that you do have options. It's easy if you haven't yet saved for retirement to give up and ignore the concept altogether. That is the worst option possible. Instead, read the next section and find an option that fits your specific circumstances. Then, set that as your goal and get moving toward it.

Choose Your Retirement Option

In this section, I provide you with various retirement options. Each scenario is dependent upon two factors: 1. The career and money choices you've made up to this point, and 2. The career and money choices you'll make going forward.

If you're in your early 20s, literally all these choices are possible for you! You just need to decide on the one that matches your needs and desires the most closely. If you're in your 40s, all options are still available to you, but you might have to institute one of the frugality options in conjunction with your preferred choice.

Option #1: Save your promotion money. When most people get a promotion, they immediately adapt their lifestyle to match their new income choice. It makes sense. They want to reward themselves for a job well done. Some want to reward their spouse or children in an effort to make up for the time spent away from the family.

You can make a different choice. Rather than spend your promotion income, each time you get a promotion, keep your same lifestyle. Don't buy a more expensive car or house because now you can afford it. Only buy what you need. Continue living on the income you were living on before your promotion. Then save the rest of your promotion money.

For example, let's say you're living on $100,000 per year, and you get a promotion moving you to $112,000 per year. You would simply save the amount you already were saving, and then add your take-home promotion money to your savings. So in this example, out of the $1,000 per month your salary increased, you might be taking home $750 of it. You'll save that $750 instead of going out to buy a more expensive car or a bigger house. After 20 years, that $750 per month will result in adding approximately $1200 per month to your retirement income.

If you get a really large raise, or if you need to pay off some of your accrued debt, you might want to split your raise into two streams. Half you would use to pay down debt or treat yourself to something special. The other half you would save. The most important strategy is to save as much of your promotion money as you can.

The advantage of saving your promotion money is twofold. The most obvious reason is that the more you save, the earlier you have the option to retire. But the other important reason has to do with your replacement income in retirement, a concept I reviewed in the last section.

If you're used to living on $100,000 per year pre-retirement, that's all you need to save for. If you start living on all of your promotion money, that's the lifestyle you'll get used to. Let's say you work your way up the ladder and are making $140,000 per year. If you're saving $40,000 of it, then you're used to living on $100,000 per year. But if you aren't saving any, that $140,000 income is the lifestyle you'll have to fund when you retire. Otherwise, it will be a big shock going from living on $140,000 per year to $100,000 per year (or less, if you haven't saved anything). Remember, for every $40,000 of replacement income in retirement, you need to save another $1 million. In short, the more expensive your lifestyle, the harder it will be to achieve an early retirement date.

Not sure if saving your promotion money is enough to achieve your desired retirement lifestyle? If you want to make about 80% of your non-retirement gross income after you quit working, use this chart below to see if you're on track. In an article for CNBC, financial expert Kimmie Greene recommends the following:

- Age 35: Have twice your annual salary saved.
- Age 40: Have three times your annual salary saved.
- Age 45: Have four times your annual salary saved.
- Age 50: Have five times your annual salary saved.
- Age 55: Have six times your annual salary saved.
- Age 60: Have seven times your annual salary saved.
- Age 65: Have eight times your annual salary saved.

Option #2: Spend your promotion money, but keep your savings rate constant. This scenario won't help your retirement savings as much as Option #1. However, it will keep you on track to retire at a reasonable age. If you want to retire around age 65, and you start saving in your 20s, most experts recommend you save a steady 10-15% of your income throughout your life. Many recommend closer to 15-20%, due to the rising cost of health care and the possibility of social security going broke before you retire.

If you save 20%-25% of your income from your 20s going forward, you will be set up well for retirement. Thus, each time you get a promotion, simply continue to save the same percentage you've saved all along. In effect, you'll be able to keep some of your promotion money while maintaining a savings rate that steadily moves you toward retirement.

For example, let's say you're making $100,000 per year, saving 20% of your income. This means your take-home is $80,000 per year. Then you get a raise to $140,000 per year. If you still save 20%, you will increase your annual savings from $20,000 per year to $28,000 per year. And your take-home pay would increase from $80,000 per year to $112,000. You're not saving all of your promotion money, and your savings rate won't move you more quickly toward retirement. But at least you'll ensure the percentage you save will increase commensurately with your more expensive lifestyle.

Option #3: Save nothing and work your entire life in your chosen profession. This option is actually the "no retirement" option. As in, work your whole life, until you die. For many people, this is not an option at all. However, consider the research. People who work longer tend to live longer. They keep their social connections. They maintain a sense of purpose. They move their bodies and use their minds, preventing a host of physical ailments.

If you have the type of job requiring some movement, but not hard labor, this option might be for you. If you would otherwise be home alone, watching TV and rarely speaking to other humans, continuing to work could enhance your longevity. The average life expectancy of women in North America is currently 81 years old. For men, it is 79. The higher your education and income level, and the healthier your lifestyle, the longer your predicted longevity.

So, it's not at all unreasonable to anticipate working into your 70s, if you want to. By then, you probably will have paid off your house, your debt, and your kids' college educations. This will make it easier for you to save some amount, at least enough to retire before your health begins to turn. Or maybe you really don't want to retire at all. You just want to work until your death. In that case, you need zero savings. Enjoy your work!

Option #4: Implement a FIRE lifestyle. F.I.R.E is an acronym that stands for "Financial Independence, Retire Early." The FIRE movement refers to a lifestyle implemented in order to retire early, whatever the definition of retire early is for you. For most people who follow the FIRE lifestyle, early retirement means by 40. For others, an early retirement could mean leaving the workforce at age 50, 55, or even 60, if their original retirement plan kept them working well beyond that.

You can find multiple blogs and social media forums with FIRE strategies and tips. There are two main steps to achieving FIRE. The first step is to institute an extremely frugal lifestyle. The benefits are twofold. First, FIRE followers learn to live on a much lower annual income. Then, because they get used to the frugal lifestyle, this annual income becomes their target replacement income in their retirement years. Reviewing the online forums, you can see that FIRE followers have learned to live on incomes that can be less than $40,000 per year.

The next step for FIRE followers is saving the remainder of their annual income. After instituting a frugal lifestyle, FIRE followers typically save 60-70% of their regular salary. This allows them to build a nest egg large enough to retire by their 40s if they began in their 20s.

The nest egg FIRE followers shoot for depends entirely on their desired retirement income. As you saw at the beginning of this chapter, you'll need to have $1 million saved for each $40,000 you want in retirement. If FIRE followers are used to living on $40,000 per year, all they need to save is $1 million. If they are used to living on $80,000 per year, then they would need to save $2 million by the time they retire.

Saving $2 million by the time you're 40 might seem like a crazy goal. But it's actually quite do-able for double-income couples who implement FIRE strategies early in their career. Imagine a couple in their early 20s, each earning $60,000 per year, or $120,000 total. They want to retire by their early 40s, living on $80,000 per year, or 67% of their joint income.

In the example below, here's how much per month they have to save as a couple in order to achieve a $2 million next egg. The chart shows their savings target per month based on how long they will save. This scenario assumes a 5% return on investment. Most stock market index funds will average a higher rate of return over 15-20 years.

- Save for 20 years: $2,500 per person ($5,000 total, 50% of salary)
- Save for 15 years: $3750 per person ($7,500 total, 75% of salary)
- Save for 10 years: Not possible on $120,000 per year, but would be $7,500 per person ($13,000 total)
- Save for 5 years: Not possible on $120,000 per year, but would be $15,000 per year ($30,000 total)

Again you can see the importance of beginning to save early. Maybe this couple later decides they wish to continue working. They would do so knowing that they have the freedom to retire at any time. They could even work part-time as their kids were being raised. And what about their kids' college fund? They could fund that while saving for retirement, simply by saving more. Or they could work an extra few years for the purpose paying for their kids' college. Either way, they will have saved early in order to have freedom later on.

Option #5: Wait to save, then institute extreme frugality and save 50% or more of your salary until you can retire. This scenario is less prescriptive than the previous options. Your own retirement outcome will be dependent upon several factors. First, you need to figure out what you actually need to live on during your retirement. Then, you need to decide if you want a larger income than what you need.

Obviously, if you haven't saved anything yet, and you're in your 40s, your options will be narrower. You might only be able to save enough to retire on the income you need to pay your bills, with very little left over. If you've saved at least some money along the way, you will have wider options in terms of how much longer you must save and the income you'll have in your retirement. In short, the longer you wait to save, the fewer retirement options you'll have.

As you know by now, your retirement savings account needs to generate enough replacement income for you in retirement. How frugal you need to be from this point on depends upon the amount you want.

Let's say you're 45, you have no retirement savings yet, and you want to retire at 60. In order to do that, as shown above, you'll need to save about $7,500 per month to generate $2 million by age 60. That will give you $80,000 in retirement. But $7,500 per month is $90,000 per year you need to save. If you're making $170,000 per year, that's 53% of your income. And you'll need to live on the remainder: $80,000 per year. And you'll be living on that from age 45 until you retire at age 60.

If before you began saving you were used to living on your full salary of $170,000 per year, that's going to feel very restrictive for you. And yet, it's the only way you can retire by 60. Keep in mind that if you don't start saving for retirement until you're 45, you'll be facing a very frugal retirement compared to the lifestyle you've been living.

But let's say you're willing to work to age 65. In that case, you don't need to cut your budget quite as much. You can save $5,000 per month, or $60,000 per year. Of your $170,000 annual income, that's still 35% of your salary. The problem is that you're shooting to make $80,000 per year in retirement. But if you're only saving $60,000 per year of our $170,000 income, you would still be used to living on $110,000. That's $30,000 more than you'll have in retirement.

So in this scenario, you have to decide for yourself—do you save more so you can boost yourself to $2.5 million in savings? That would get you $100,000 per year in retirement. Do you save everything you can so you can get used to living on $80,000 per year? Do you work until you're 70?

The reason it's important to review this scenario is that some people simply cannot, or will not, save for their retirement in their 20s and 30s. Studies show that, if they save at all for retirement, most people only have about 12-15% of what they'll need. If that's you, then analyze your lifestyle spending choices. Decide what will need to change in retirement. If you're like most Americans, you're going to need to drastically reduce your spending and live on a much leaner household budget if you've delayed saving into your 40s. If a strict, budget-conscious retirement lifestyle is what you're preparing for, you might as well start saving and living very frugally now.

Option #6: Phase your retirement. If you can't afford to retire fully at the age you want, you might want to phase your retirement. What this means is that you would retire from your higher-paying, higher-pressure job. Then you would continue to work full time, but in a less stressful job.

For example, let's say you already have $1 million saved, but you need about $1.5 million to retire. At 5% interest, if you simply let your $1 million grow, without adding anything to it, you'd have $1.5 million in about 8 years.

So what you would look for in a phased retirement is a job that pays you only what you need to live on, without saving. If you're making $100,000 per year, saving 20% of that, that means you're used to living on $80,000. If you can find a less stressful job making $80,000 per year, you would take it as your last phase of working before you retire. Again, you would simply let your savings up to that point grow.

If you have a particularly accommodating employer, you might be able to reduce your salary by 20% and work only 4 days a week. If you have specific skills others want, you might be able to consult instead of work full time. And, if you are willing to live on even less than $80,000 per year, you would have more options. You could take an easier job. Work less. Or save more so that the 8 remaining years of working ends up as only 6 more years.

Another option is to spend your last 5 years working for a government or educational employer that vests retirement in 5 years, so that you get a small pension later in life. The more applicable to government work your current work is, the better chance you'll have using this option.

Private industry careers in finance, accounting, facilities, human resources, safety/security, secretarial-clerical and project planning typically translate well to government careers. Also, if you're in a geographic area where there is a shortage of teachers, you can usually participate in a free (or low-cost) "alternative route to teacher licensure" program. These programs help you become a teacher in a short time period.

For example, let's say you're a Vice President of Facilities for a large corporation. You have to be focused on cost savings, revenue, customer service scores, and a myriad of other issues that make your life stressful. If you get a facilities job working for a city or school district, your job is likely to be less stressful. You'll make less money, for sure. But if you work there for 5-10 years, you'll most likely be eligible for a small pension, usually beginning at age 65. And you'll just let your savings up to that point grow.

There are many other versions of phased retirements. Some retirees only want to earn a little extra travel money, so they take very easy, part-time jobs with no stress involved.

It's not uncommon these days to see retirees working in fast food restaurants, in department stores, and in fitness centers. If you can't fully retire, but you want an easier job, a phased retirement is for you.

Option #7: Institute a working retirement. This is similar to a phased retirement, except you don't ever quit working entirely. A working retirement might sound like a terrible idea to you. However, it's actually becoming more and more common for several reasons. Many people simply never save for retirement. In that case, they have no option but to continue working in some capacity. That is certainly unfortunate; you always want to work toward having *some* options.

You can institute a working retirement in a less-stressful job, even if it's part-time. And, you can achieve enormous physical and psychological benefits by continuing to work well into what would normally be considered retirement age.

Too many retirees fail to exercise, walk, or even stand throughout the day. They have limited social connections. They no longer learn new things. They quit reading in favor of watching TV. They eat more, including more processed food. They drink more alcohol than they should. These are all activities that increase the aging process, contribute to diseases, are linked to many cancers, and are associated with Alzheimer's disease and dementia.

Sure, you might engage in all of those activities while still working. But if you continue working, you're less likely to do so. Just be sure that where you work isn't a stressful environment. Choose a job working somewhere you enjoy. If you can't find that, check out a temp agency. There, you can work in a variety of roles for several different companies. Don't like one of the places? Ask to work elsewhere in the future.

Other options for less stressful, continued work during retirement include running your own small business, consulting in your area of expertise, working for fast food or retail stores, and working for events that need additional temporary workers such as conventions, concerts, tournaments and large community gatherings.

Follow the Dos and Don'ts for a Wealthy Retirement

Now that you know how much to save, and all of the different options for your retirement, here are 15 Dos and Don'ts to retire wealthy—whatever that number means to you. Keep these at the top of your mind by posting them somewhere you are forced to look at each day. They will keep you focused regardless of your own retirement decisions. All contain good advice no matter what age you begin your retirement savings journey.

Do decide how much is enough. This is the first, and most important piece of advice. If you fail to do this, you will never get yourself on track, or back on track. Even if you are 60 years old reading this book, do it immediately. Decide right now the retirement lifestyle you want and what is do-able for your savings timeline. Calculate how much you need to save each year.

Do educate yourself. This book provided you with a thorough baseline of knowledge. But you need to find and use a retirement planning calculator to solidify and verify your numbers and assumptions. If you have a Fidelity account, theirs is my favorite because you can put in so many variables during retirement. Most other investment banks have something similar. You can also find free savings and retirement calculators online. Just google "retirement savings calculator" to find them.

Don't keep up with the Jones's. Many studies have shown that rich doctors have among the highest amount of consumer debt, and the lowest average savings (relative to income) of any profession. How could that be? The theory is that it's because they feel as if they need to keep up with the "doctor" lifestyle. Their friends all drive sports cars, so why don't they?

This is a common problem. If you try to match your lifestyle to friends who make the same amount of money you do, you'll never be on track to save what you need. Make saving for retirement cool among your group of friends. Don't be afraid to say, "I'd rather retire at 45 than buy a new car" or "The size of our house is perfect right now. We'd rather save for retirement than have a higher mortgage."

Do hire someone if you won't do it yourself. You need to hire a financial planning professional if you simply refuse to plan for your own retirement. Be careful, however. Most of the planning professionals take a percentage of your savings as an Assets Under Management (AUM) fee. Some are getting paid commissions by the mutual fund companies themselves. Most take a combination of both. These fees can influence the advisor's judgment regarding how to invest your money. In addition, most studies show that the vast majority of advisors don't earn you any higher investment returns than you would make investing in an index fund yourself.

I recommend you find a fee-only advisor if you don't feel comfortable investing yourself. These advisors don't earn any commissions from investments. Instead, they charge you an hourly rate, typically $200-$400 per hour. They have the lowest conflict of interest when offering advice.

Depending on their ongoing involvement in your finances, fee-only advisors might also charge an overall AUM fee as well. Again, that will greatly reduce your total savings over a lifetime. One study explained at NerdWallet.com estimated that a 1% fee could cost millennials $590,000 over their lifetime. That was based on adding $10,000 per year at a 7% return.

If you don't want to handle it yourself, find a fee-only advisor and pay him/her once per year to review your goals and provide advice. Then manage your money yourself. If you won't save at all unless someone is doing all the work for you, it's better to pay a solid financial planning professional to do it for you, regardless of fees. Just be sure to get referrals and compare fees across professionals.

Don't put your head in the sand. After several difficult years with no savings, some people pretend there isn't a problem. Know this: if you aren't planning for some sort of retirement, it's always a problem. You can't just pretend you'll never age. Even if you've had a severe financial setback, you can still plan.

In my career coaching, I find that people are reluctant to plan for worst-case scenarios. It's as if they hope that if they don't think about a negative outcome, it will never happen. But sometimes it does. I'm a big proponent in thinking positively and visioning your best-case scenario. But I also believe you must have back-up plans if something happens to derail you from your goals.

Having multiple plans is helpful for two reasons. First, if the worst happens, it's less stressful. You already know that if "A" happens, you have options. Having options relieves your brain from worry. It's true maybe you don't love your options. But you'll ease your stress if you see a pathway to the future. Second, having another option is practical. When you know exactly what you'll do if a worst-case scenario occurs, you won't make mistakes at the outset. Your brain will automatically know the exact steps you should take.

In short, keep your eyes wide open. Know your options, good or bad. Begin planning so you know what you'll do. If your only option is to continue working, then plan now. Get the experiences and make the contacts you'll need to have multiple opportunities as you age.

Don't rely on Social Security. This is a tip provided by most retirement professionals. Social Security is a great benefit that will increase your monthly retirement income. However, who knows if it will actually be available when you plan to retire? It's difficult to imagine a world without Social Security, but you have to plan for it happening. If you're young and think that your retirement will be paid for by Social Security, think again.

First, Social Security alone is not enough to pay for your living expenses, unless you'll be living in poverty during your retirement. Second, the age you can access it, and the benefits associated with it, are likely to become more and more restrictive. Many analysts predict our government won't be able to afford it in the future. To be safe, plan to fund your own retirement. Then, Social Security will be a pleasant surprise when it becomes available to you.

Don't rely on an inheritance or other money windfall. Never rely on an outside source to fund your retirement. When you rely on others as a source of income, you're likely to be disappointed. Parents don't always give you accurate information about their finances. If they do, sometimes situations occur that even they haven't planned for. They get divorced. They spend their money on medical expenses. They make a bad investment. If you get a windfall from your parents or other sources, consider it a nice blessing. It can change your retirement plans for the better, for sure. Just don't rely on it to fund your preferred retirement option.

Don't fall for get rich quick schemes. Sometimes it's easy to fall for a fabulous opportunity that looks like it will make you money fast. Yes, some opportunities really are great deals. Some are not. Don't risk your retirement savings on any unproven investments. If you really think there is a good opportunity you can't pass up, risk only the amount you can afford to lose. Don't give any investment the power to change your retirement date.

Do diversify. As any financial advisor will tell you, you must diversify your investments. You may be getting stock options from the fabulous company you work for. Still, when those options vest, you should ensure you've diversified appropriately.

There are several ways to diversify your investments. You can diversify between types of mutual funds, such as international, US, large company stocks, small company stocks, and bonds. You can diversify your own stock choices by buying stock from multiple sectors such as hospitality, transportation, energy, technology, and fuel.

One of my favorite, and easy, ways to diversify is to buy what is called a retirement strategy or target date mutual fund. You simply decide what your retirement year is likely to be. Then you choose the fund that matches it. Then the professionals diversify your investments, changing them from riskier to less risky as you get closer to retirement.

The advantage is that you can save it and forget it without having to reallocate your portfolio as you age. However, be sure that your own retirement strategy fund performs as well as, or better, than others. Also, go with what is called a no load fund, which will greatly reduce the fees you pay over time.

Do consider index funds. Index funds seek to match the overall market over time. The advantage of an index fund is that you're leaving very little to chance in regard to your returns over time. You don't have to worry about renegade investment leaders trying to beat the market and losing.

Index funds offer low risk within each investment category. This is because the only goal is to match the market. It makes it somewhat easier for the mutual fund manager because he/she can mimic the market in terms of what individual stocks are chosen. There is not a lot of guessing involved. Of course unanticipated issues can occur with individual companies or market sectors. Still, index funds offer the best bet to ensure your money earns at least average returns over time.

Do use automatic withdrawals. You've probably heard the phrase "Pay yourself first." Automatic withdrawals do that for you. You will do a better job consistently saving for your retirement if you never see your money before it gets deposited into your retirement account.

Set up your paycheck so that your employer pays the appropriate savings accounts before your paycheck is issued. Doing so, you will be forced to budget for your income after saving. This will keep you disciplined each time you are paid.

When you get a pay raise, allow yourself to be paid one paycheck so that you can see the increase to your pay after taxes. Then add the exact amount of the increase to your savings going forward. If you continually increase your savings this way, you will greatly increase your chances to retire early.

Do maximize your tax-deferred savings options. The IRS provides a number of savings options that defer or reduce your tax burden as you save. Always choose some sort of tax-deferred option whenever you can. Doing so will net you more money in the long run. The amount you're saving, but would otherwise be paying to Uncle Sam, really adds up over time. Each savings option has its own benefits. Sometimes your employer or your company match contributions, so you should always choose that type of account first.

Your specific situation will determine the pros and cons of each option. Do your research. Seek advice if you need to. The account types you'll want to consider are the 401k, the 403b (for education and non-profits), the 401a, the 457 (for government and education), the IRA or Roth IRA, and the 529 (college savings). Find out what's right for you, and maximize those savings options first.

Don't accrue consumer debt. Don't accrue consumer debt. The only debt you should have is your house. Consumer debt is when individuals can't afford to live within their budget. They spend more than they make, using a credit card. Consumer debt usually carries a high interest rate. But that's not the most important problem.

The most important problem is that use of consumer debt to pay for monthly expenses that have no return/equity (such as your house) has a negative snowball effect on your budget. What seems like a relatively small $500 overage one month can snowball exponentially if you never learn how to save and budget.

Consumer debt also wreaks havoc on disciplined budgeting. If you overspend by $500 one month, you have to reduce that $500 in your budget the following month, just to get back on track. In that way, you're never addressing the root of the problem, which is your overspending. And that also makes it even more difficult for you if you lose your job. You'll have bills to pay that go well beyond normal living costs.

There are always going to be unanticipated expenses. You should have enough money saved up in cash to pay for them. If you've already accrued a significant amount of consumer debt, commit to yourself that you'll get back on track.

Target one bill to pay off, while making the minimum payment on others. Reduce other items in your budget until you can pay it off. Then, once it's paid off, roll over that payment onto the next credit card, and so on, until you're debt-free.

Do drive your car for several years (and never lease a car). Some people don't consider a car payment to be consumer debt. I do. New or old, cars don't appreciate in value. In my view, they use a large chunk of your monthly income that you could be putting toward savings. And, if you lease a car, you'll never be without a car payment because you own nothing.

You should always seek to buy the most reliable used car you can find, at the lowest price. Don't get a car you can afford. Get only the car you need. Check out Consumer Reports' annual issue about cars that are three years old. It's a valuable resource for finding a great used car at a reasonable price.

Because I'd rather save for retirement than have a car payment, I drive a car that is 12 years old and has 130,000 miles on it. It's a great brand, in great condition. My mechanic says I can easily drive it for another 70,000 miles. I bought it new, something pretty much no smart saver—including me—recommends doing. I had a car payment for 5 years before it was paid off. I've had no car payment for 7 years, and I like it that way.

Ideally, you should be saving money specifically for the purpose of buying a car in the future. If you buy a reliable car at a good price, you can make that payment while also saving for your next car. Let's say you have a $500 car payment for 5 years. On top of that, you save $250 per month.

After your car is paid off in five years, you start saving $750 per month, the exact amount in your budget you were allocating toward your car when you had a payment. At the end of the initial 5 years, you will have saved $250 per month, totaling $15,000. Then, if you save another $750 per month for three years, that's another $27,000. After 8 years of driving your car, you will have saved $42,000 to buy your next car—if you even want to spend that much!

No matter how many promotions you get, if you fail to save for your retirement, you won't have a chance of retiring early. This chapter explained how you can analyze your own needs and desires for retirement. I made clear how you can decide your ideal retirement age, and how much you want to save during each step of your career. I gave you several retirement options to consider based on your decisions in the past and those you will make in the future. Finally, I listed 15 dos and don'ts that will help guide you on your path to early retirement. I hope you can use the strategies in this chapter to put your promotion money to good use. If you won't do it yourself, find a professional who will!

Conclusion

This book provided you with ten strategies you can use to get promoted, make more money, and retire wealthy—all without risking your own money to be an entrepreneur! You can put your new knowledge to use immediately, whether you're a recent college graduate or a seasoned professional.

Your future success will be dependent upon your commitment. Begin working on one new strategy a month. Then layer on the next strategy, and so on. Within one year, you'll be using all ten strategies so well, you will no longer have to think about them. And you'll be well on your way to a successful career and a wealthy retirement.

Want some individual career coaching along the way? Just email me at stacimcintosh23@gmail.com. I'm happy to answer any initial questions via a free phone consultation.

Want To Know More?

If you want more information on this topic, The Anti-Entrepreneur Book Two provides equally practical advice. In it, I describe in detail eight very important criteria you should use to choose the right job. If you're a new professional or if you're making a career change, you'll learn how to make a big difference in your income just by choosing the right employer. You'll learn the specific factors to consider, and you'll learn the smart choices you need to make along the way. Choosing the right employer, and the right type of job, is one of the most critical aspects of ensuring a successful career trajectory. It's available now, so check it out on Amazon! The Anti-Entrepreneur Book Three will also be available soon. It will teach you how to avoid the common mistakes that will slow your advancement or derail your chances for promotion.

If you're searching for a job and want focused help regarding the process, I also provide job search advice through the One Hour Handbook Series. The books below are packed with useful help about resumes, applications, job interviews and involuntary job losses. Read them, and you will perform well above your competition no matter what reason you're looking for a new job.

Job Search Passport: Using Industry Secrets to Write Applications, Resumes and Cover Letters

Ready for Take-Off: Preparing for Interview Questions on Your Job Search Journey

Wheels Up: Mastering the Job Interview to Launch Your Career

Brace for Landing: Managing Your Life and Career After Being Laid Off, Fired, Pushed Out or Demoted

Finally, as I shared earlier, if you have a specific question about your particular situation, you can always email me at stacimcintosh23@gmail.com. I love to hear from people like you! Also, if my advice helped you, I would really appreciate you leaving a few positive comments via an Amazon review.

Connect with Staci McIntosh to get free advice and receive updates on her upcoming books.

Email: stacimcintosh23@gmail.com
LinkedIn: Staci (Vesneske) McIntosh
Facebook: @mcintoshbooks, Job Search and Career Advice
Twitter: @StaciVegas

If you find Staci's advice helpful, please leave an Amazon book review before you go.

www.ingramcontent.com/pod-product-compliance
Lightning Source LLC
Chambersburg PA
CBHW020433220526
45464CB00002B/686